- for Brooke -

I'D DO IT ALL AGAIN. THREE TIMES.
BUT ONLY IF YOU COME WITH ME.

Acknowledgments

Most of the time, I skip over the acknowledgments section in a book. I just want to get to the part where the story is interesting. Or where the information is something that I want to learn. And, dear reader, this may very well be a boring section for you to read. But it is my favorite section to write.

Because it's about my people. My friends. My team. And I know that you probably don't know these people. But you should. And that's why I'm going to share a bit about them with you.

Thank you to Holly - you've been there every step of the way. Through all of it. From the playground, to boyfriends, college, death, marriage, birth and divorce. You've seen me through more things than most people see in a lifetime.

To Tina - my battle buddy. We've laid in the same muddy trench, protected each other from enemy fire, and have come back home stronger and better.

Someday, we will sit around laughing. Swapping war stories with the younger moms. And we will look at each other. And smile.

To James - thank you for waking me back up to adventure. Highway 20 rides, flea markets, bull rides and country music. Life wouldn't be the same without you.

To Kaitlyn - my niece, my friend. You've been my money muse, worthy opponent in the Rat Race, and oh So Money. Thank you for the inspiration, the laughs, and the listening. For your fierce loyalty and love. Most of all, for being there in those quiet, private hours with me and my girl. You're more than my friend. You're my family.

To Zeke - so much more than just a cabana boy. I'm proud to call you my friend. To watch you become who you really are. Thank you for being here for me and for my girl. For always bringing us a smile and a laugh. For being strong when I needed to feel safe. For being part of the house that built me and built you too.

To Isabelle - my girl. I love you. The fire in your spirit, the light in your eyes, makes me want to be a better person. To live up to what I'm called to do. Honey, you are going places. Big, bright, beautiful places. And I am so proud to be your mama.

To Brooke. I started to write my friend, but that word just isn't big enough to describe who you are to me. You know who you are to me. I know you speak it. This book wouldn't exist without your work. I wouldn't be who I am today without your friendship. Thank you for seeing who I really am. (Even when I made it almost impossible). And for letting me in on that little secret. And for helping me get here. I love you.

To You - my teachers, my clients, my students, my Rowdies, and my readers. I am so honored to be able to share with you and learn from you. Thank you.

Table Of Contents

Foreword

This is a book about loving money. And no. Loving money is not the root of all evil. Evil is the root of all evil. Money just makes evil more evil. But it also makes love more lovely. Generosity more possible. And you, more able to express who you already are.

What we do with our money matters.

We spend our lives slaving away for it.

We marry for it.

We placate our bosses to get it.

We sacrifice time with our families for more of it.

And then we pretend it doesn't matter.

We pretend we have it when we don't.

Car Leases. Balloon mortgages. Citibank Credit Cards.

We don't want anyone to know how much we make or how much we spend. We want to make sure people think we are smart with it. And we most definitely want to ensure that we are sensitive with other people who have "not so much" of it.

But when it comes to telling the truth about it. Well, we don't. We lie to ourselves, our spouses and our friends about what we can afford and how much we make and save.

This book is about coming clean with your money and with yourself. It's about love. Loving yourself enough to tell the truth. Loving yourself enough to earn, save and spend money in a way that serves your highest good on the planet. It's about understanding that how you do money is an example of how you do your life. It's about having a relationship with money that feels amazing.

Meadow has created the tools to get it done. Don't just read this book. Do this book. Tell the truth and open yourself up to the possibility that changing your relationship to money can change your entire life. It can teach you things you may not have known about who you are and who you genuinely want to be.

I have been profoundly changed by this work: I have watched client after client release ideas and beliefs that keep them in broke denial in exchange for beliefs and ideas that allow not only for long term wealth, but more importantly, peace and truth around money. You too, deserve peace and love when it comes to your money. Use what you learn here to get it.

-*Brooke Castillo*
March 2011

Why You Shouldn't Listen to Me

I am not a financial advisor. I am not an accountant. I'm not even a bookkeeper.

I've never worked on Wall Street. Or in a bank.

I didn't go to a fancy school. I got my degree in plain-ol' physics and math from a tiny school in North Lake Tahoe. I never once took a class in finance.

I don't wear a suit or high heels to work. In fact, most of the time I work in yoga clothes with no shoes on.

I don't have a diverse financial portfolio. But, I used to have quite a diverse credit card portfolio. One in every color.

I have made way more mistakes with money than you ever have.

I lived beyond my means for all of my twenties and most of my thirties.

I bought my last two houses at the highest point of the California market. And then waited until the very worst moment in recent real estate history to get a divorce and split assets (and when I say assets... I mean debt).

In 2008, I was 35 years old and over a half-million dollars in debt. Now it is 2011, and I have paid off all but $25,000.

I know what it feels like to stress about money. I've spent most of my life with that terrible feeling in my stomach. I know what money stress does to a person, to a business, to a marriage, to a family.

I know what it's like to not sleep at night.

I know the guilt and anxiety that comes from

over-spending. I know how awful it feels to be out of control.

I know what it's like to think something is wrong with you. To wish you could fix whatever is broken.

I know the fear of not knowing where the next dollar is going to come from. Or how the bills are going to get paid.

I know what it's like to be scared of being found out. To be scared of people knowing that I was a fake. A fraud. To frantically try to keep the facade going. And to try to be better than I was.

I know what it's like to be exhausted. And to want to give up.

Hoping to be saved.

And...

I also know what it's like to have survived this. To save myself.

I know what it's like to be strong. Courageous.

I know what it's like to take responsibility for my life. For my finances.

I know what it's like to start from scratch. Again.

And win.

I know what it's like to love myself. To forgive myself. To understand myself. To have compassion for my past choices.

I know what it's like to help people like me and like you out of financial hell.

If we could sit down together, you could look into my eyes and if you looked closely enough, you would see that I have felt your same pain.

And, because of this. You are my friend.

And because you're my friend, I have decided to write a book for you. And if this book saves you from even one moment of unnecessary suffering. Then I have done my job.

But, please don't listen to me.

I didn't write this book with that intention.

I wrote it for you to listen to yourself.

Take what's right for you.

And leave the rest.

Chapter 1

How to Love Money

Do you love money?

Are you sure?

If you're anything like me, or my clients, we've actually had to learn how to love money.

I used to think I loved money because I could spend it. I loved what money could buy. I loved the stuff that could be purchased with it. I loved the adventures that money could take me on. I loved the idea of shopping or spending.

So many of my clients have this same belief.

Money is only good for what it can buy. Money is as good as what can be purchased with it.

To make it really simple.

The way I loved money was to get rid of it. And fast.

And, this.

Is not love.

We love our kids, right? And we don't want to give them away. (Ok, maybe sometimes we do want to give them away. But for the sake of the metaphor... follow me on this). We want to spend time with them, take care of them, and protect them.

We love our pets. We don't get a puppy just so that we can quickly exchange it for something else. (Alright, maybe this isn't the best metaphor, either. But, hopefully you'll get the gist). We love spending time with our pets, taking care of them, playing with them, and protecting them.

What if we loved money—in the same way that we love our kids?

What if we loved our money by spending time with it (saving it), taking care of it (investing wisely) and protecting it (not buying shit that we don't want and we don't need).

What if we respected our relationship with money—just like we respect our relationship with people that we care about? What if we treated it like something that meant a lot to us?

What if we saw spending money that we don't have (going into debt) in the same way that we would see having affairs with people who aren't our partners.

What if we saw debt as **cheating** on our own money? My best friend says, "I love money."

Often.
Out loud.
To strangers.

And she really means it. She's the one who

showed me what the love of money really means. She respects it. She loves to make it. She loves to hang out with it. She loves to give it, share it, keep it.

I want you to love money.

I want you to love **your** money.

Care for it. Respect it. Hang out with it. Take care of it.

It's yours.

You earned it.

Chapter 2

It's Time to Change Your Mind

Whether we want to earn more, or spend less, or get out of debt, or save more, or worry less. If we want to have a better relationship with money, there's only one thing we need to do to create lasting change.

Change our mind.

It's not more complicated than that. We don't have to understand investments, banking, real estate, business, dividends, stocks, ROI's, percentages, budgets, spreadsheets or exchange rates. We only need to understand the way our mind works.

And, by the way… that's a big 'only.'

Money is a neutral thing. It can be proven to exist or not exist. It's a fact. It's a number. It can be a number on paper. It can be a number on your computer screen. It can be a number on a receipt. It can be a number on a dollar bill in your wallet.

This money, this number, doesn't hold any power on its own. It has no emotional charge. It can't create pain and it can't create pleasure. It's just a number. The only power it has is the power we give it. And we give it power through our stories.

And, boy-oh-boy, can we tell a good story about these numbers. We tell stories about not having enough of these numbers. We tell stories about how these numbers never stay with us. We tell stories saying how hard we work for these numbers. How difficult these numbers are. How painful these numbers are. We tell stories that we aren't given enough of these numbers. That other people are given more of these numbers. If we only had more of these numbers we would feel better. Happier. Smarter. Safer. Hell, even sexier.

These stories roll around in our head—day and night—and they hold a lot of power over our bodies, our actions and our lives. When we believe a stressful story, our brain tells our body to feel stress. This has nothing to do with the validity of the story. Whether our story is fiction or truth. Our bodies are servants to our minds. Our bodies respond with emotion. Stress, anxiety, overwhelmingness, worry, anger, hopelessness, fear, despair or joy, excitement, optimism, hope. Our bodies respond to the stories that we tell ourselves.

While we are feeling these emotions we live our lives.

These feelings determine the way we act, and they color the way we do what we do. With these feelings, we are constantly doing things.

Buying things.
Selling things.
Building things.
Destroying things.
Avoiding things.
Pretending things.
Drinking things.

Eating things.

Watching things.

Ignoring things.

And, these 'doings' add up to significant results. These actions can create results of success or failure, of wealth or poverty, of savings or debt, of connection or disconnection. These actions can make us richer. They can also make us poorer.

If you look around your life and do not like the results you see. If you'd like to have more money, or less debt, or a better job, or a higher salary, or more money in savings:

You have to change your thinking.

That's where I come in. I help with that big "only" of changing your mind. Changing your mind takes practice. Most of us were never taught how to think. We weren't taught that our thinking leads to every result in our life. We weren't taught what to do with a negative thought or a negative feeling. We weren't taught to change our mind when we can't change our circumstances. We weren't taught that we have the choice to feel better—no matter what is happening around us.

These are skills to learn, understand, and practice.

You can learn how to change your mind. You can change those old programs that you've been running in the background of your financial life; and you can permanently change the way you think about money.

I've seen hundreds of my clients change their thinking, and I've seen the life changing results from their work. I've done this work, and continue to do this work, and have lived the results myself.

They've done it. I've done it. And I know you can too.

Join us.

Chapter 3

What We Really Want

We say we want more money. We say we'd like to win the lottery. A better paying job, a bonus, or a raise. We say we'd like our stocks to go up, or our house to sell. More clients, better investments or passive income. We say we'd like a windfall, or a book deal.

I used to say things like that, too. I used to say that I wanted more money, more clients, a better house, better car, more vacations and more clothes.

But now I know that this isn't what I really want. (Except for the clothes, of course... I still want those.) What I really want is the freedom that I think the lottery would give me.

The security from the better job.
The pride from the bonus.
The confidence from the raise.
The safety of higher stocks.
The independence of selling the house.
The stability of more clients.
The ease of passive income.
The relaxation of the windfall.
The honor of a book deal.

Ok... and... (sigh) what I really want is how I think those clothes are going to make me feel. (Cashmere does feel good. Trust.)

What we really want is to feel.

Something.

And we use the idea of money as a reason to feel that emotion.

We spend huge chunks of our lives waiting for these events to happen. For circumstances to change. For the windfall to arrive at our doorstep.

The problem with this strategy is that we're not in charge of how the universe operates. Believe me...I've tried—and it doesn't seem to listen to my rules.

We aren't in charge of where the winning ticket is purchased.

We can't climb inside the boss's head and make her offer us a better job.

We don't have access to other people's checking accounts.

We can't make the stock market behave.

Or force people to buy our house.

We can't command a client to sign up with us.

Or coerce our investments to pay us what we want. And, we can't snap our fingers and have a windfall arrive on our doorstep.

Basically, if we are waiting for the stars to align so that we have more money, so that we can feel better...

We are screwed.

So, I'm suggesting an easier solution.

What we really want is a feeling. Honestly, we just want to feel better. Feelings are created in response to our thoughts.

The reason why the lottery, the job, the raise, the bonus, the windfall 'feels' better is because we would think better. When we think better thoughts, we feel better.

Security, freedom, peace, confidence, etc. are all feelings that we experience in our bodies—Cashmere is a feeling we feel on our bodies...but I digress. Each one of those feelings is a response to specific thoughts that we believe.

If we want to feel secure—we need to believe secure thoughts. We need to believe that we are safe. The money doesn't make us safe—our thoughts about the money make us safe.

We have the power to feel everything that we want. Right now.

Without even winning the lottery.

We can feel secure. We can feel free. We can feel peace. We can feel confident. And nothing even has to change, except for our mind.

Not in a woo-woo way. Not in a Yoda Jedi-Master kind of way. We aren't talking about making things levitate or appear out of nothing.

This is a very literal and real approach to getting what you want.

Realize the feeling you're looking for.   Find a thought to believe that creates that feeling.

If you want to feel secure, find evidence of safety around you. Know that you are only ever as secure as you believe you are. True security is the belief of safety.   Knowing that no matter what happens—you will always be OK.

If you want to feel free, find evidence of freedom in your life. Search for it. Free yourself from your mental prison and you will experience true freedom.

Most of the work I do with my clients is the tedious work of finding and proving new thoughts. Finding beliefs that create suffering and changing them to beliefs that feel better. We cut out the middleman. We skip the lottery, the raise, the money and we find peace now. We find freedom now.

It takes practice. It takes discipline.

And it works.

Chapter 4

Getting Ready to Open Your Eyes

To permanently change our relationship with money, we have to be willing to open our eyes. We need to know—in detail—where we stand financially. We need to take responsibility for our past and present behaviors. And, most importantly, we need to understand why we have created this financial reality. As you can probably imagine, unveiling these truths and digging through our money beliefs can be difficult, time consuming, scary, disappointing and exhausting.

But the alternative is so much worse. Believe me. I know because I've done it.

Pretending that we know where we really stand.

Keeping ourselves in the dark from the truth. Hiding from our own money. Trying to fudge the details, guessing, estimating, or fantasizing, only prolongs our dysfunctional relationship with money.

I was the queen of denial when it came to my finances. I always felt like I had a 'pretty good' idea of what was going on financially. To placate my anxiety, I'd minimize my spending and exaggerate my earning. I'd tell myself that the details really weren't that important. I thought I knew the basics, the general idea. I had a hazy idea of what I made, what I owed and what I spent.

At least that's what I told myself.

And it was a total lie.

A healthy relationship with money is vital to creating lasting abundance. The way we treat it, if we respect it, how we value it, what we do with it. Just like any other relationship in our life, our relationship with money can only be healthy if it's based on honesty, authenticity, and trust.

And money always tells the truth.

So the dysfunction in this relationship—is always our own.

Recognizing my part in this dysfunctional relationship was both daunting and freeing. Daunting because I knew I could no longer blame my divorce, my job, the economy, special circumstances, or bad luck. By relinquishing blame, I took full responsibility for my past, present and future. Once I took responsibility, I realized that I could turn the dysfunction around. I was free to create a better relationship with money. But I knew it would take work, practice and consistency.

Now, I know every minute detail. I know where my money goes and where it comes from. I know why I spend what I spend and I know why I earn what I earn. My relationship with money is grounded in reality. I'm no longer spinning stories or trying to sell myself my own cheap propaganda.

At our first session, I tell my clients that the entire first week is devoted to getting prepared to do the work ahead. Getting prepared to know the truth about where they really are. Preparing them emotionally for the challenges of this work. We don't just dive into the hard cold facts. They prepare for what they are about to learn about themselves, their past, and their beliefs.

I tell them, "There's a reason you are where you are. There's a reason why you have money—or you don't. There's a reason why you're in debt— or not. There's a reason that you're earning what you're earning and spending what you're spending."

Most of us have avoided looking at the truth of our financial situation. We avoid our bank statements, our bills, our credit card balances, our pay-off amounts. We avoid checking our accounts and live with the panic and anxiety of the not-knowing. We swipe our credit cards and secretly cross our fingers hoping that the purchase is authorized.

We tell ourselves little lies.
It's no big deal.
I'm sure its fine.
I'll deal with it later.

We avoid the details. The truth. We don't want to know what's really going on. We are kind of like that little two-year-old who covers her eyes and thinks she's invisible. But, the numbers exists whether or not we're looking.

Numbers are just numbers. They aren't personal. This isn't a judgment about who you are. It's not about how well-behaved you've been, how smart, stupid, naughty or kind you've been. It's about knowing the truth.

Chapter 5

Beliefs That Justify Avoiding the Truth

We all know that we should pay attention to our finances. We should know what we spent our money on. We should know how much is in our bank. Or how much we need to save. Or how much we need to pay.

For years, I avoided my own financial truth. I postponed checking my accounts. Thoughts about logging into my online banking would produce a painful pit in my stomach. I just didn't want to know. I wouldn't open letters (over draft notices) from my bank. I knew what they were—I'd just file them. I wouldn't open my investment statements. I'd let my credit card statements sit there until the due date, never looking at the finance charge I was paying, ignoring the list of transactions, only looking at the minimum payment amount. Crumpled up dollar bills would find their way through the laundry. I'd throw away important receipts. I'd misplace warranty information I had no idea how much cash I had (or didn't have) in my wallet.

I realize that this makes no sense. I knew, logically, that looking at my checking account balance online was not going to strike me blind. I knew that the overdrafts were costing me money that I really didn't have. I knew that my credit cards and lines of credit were charging me enormous amounts of money. I knew that avoiding it wasn't really going to fix it. At the same time, anytime I even thought about my money, or my lack of money, or my debt, I was seized with panic, worry, guilt and shame.

So, I justified avoiding the truth.

I've done this. My clients have done this. And you've probably done this, too. We think about 'dealing' with reality—and it seems too painful—so we come up with fancy reasons to avoid it.

Here are a few of the most common beliefs:

"I don't want to give negative thoughts any power." We think that we need to avoid looking at the truth, because we tell ourselves that the truth is 'negative'. It's not true. Our story about the truth is negative. The truth is never negative. The only way to dissolve a negative thought's power is to actually look at it. Write it down. Question it. Allowing negative thoughts to live in the background of your life only amplify their power.

"This will hurt my (Law of) Attraction." This is a favorite among my clients who think they understand (but don't really) the Law of Attraction. They ask me, *"won't looking at the reality of my debt just create more debt?"* The answer is no. The Law of Attraction is based on feelings. You become a match to what you feel. You attract more of what you feel. So, if you're not dealing with your debt, and you feel anxious—you can only be attracting more anxiety. Dealing with reality and with the truth always feels better. When you feel better you attract more of that feeling.

"I won't be able to overcome it." Sometimes, we have

an irrational fear that if we really know how bad our finances are—we might literally keel over dead or have an emotional breakdown or some other drastic event might happen. I had this fear and didn't even realize it. It's like being scared of the boogey man. The fear is very real. The thing you're scared of, though, doesn't exist.

Knowing the truth always feels better than avoiding it. Even when the truth seems awful, even if the truth means bankruptcy, foreclosure or worse. Avoiding the truth will only keep you stuck. The only way you will be able to overcome it and move on is to be willing to look at the truth, deal with the truth, and take action from that place.

"It will get worse." As with any relationship, our relationship with money only gets worse if we ignore it. Paying attention to it, understanding it and telling the truth about it, can only improve our relationship.

"It's not repairable." (*"It's too late." "It's too far gone."*) This is a big lie that keeps us stuck in dysfunction. We tell ourselves that we're screwed anyway, so might as well keep the blinders on. Each of us has our own

relationship with money. And each of these relationships can be repaired. No matter how drastic the mistakes are. It is always repairable.

"I'll feel even worse." This is partially true. Even though numbers are neutral, our thoughts about them can be very painful. And these thoughts can make us feel worse. That's why thought work is critical. Without it, we just suffer. If we avoid our financial reality, though, we never give ourselves the gift of bringing these painful thoughts to the surface. They just run in the backgrounds of our minds, unquestioned.

"I already know it's a mess." This was one of my personal favorites. I knew my financial life was a mess, but I wanted to just skip through the whole 'details, numbers, reality' stuff and get to the part where I just made more money. This thought will never create more abundance, though. Knowing it's a mess and understanding exactly why it's a mess are two very different things.

"I don't want to have to deprive myself." ("I don't want to be punished.") This is probably the single-

most common belief among the money-dysfunctional. So, I'm going to say, right off the bat, I never put my clients on a budget and I never tell them they can't spend money. And I don't want you to put yourself on a budget or tell yourself that you can't spend money. Budgets and white-knuckling just don't work. Forced willpower always ends up backfiring, and we end up spending even more money. Depriving us even more. This is a fascinating cycle and I'll talk more about this later.

"It's easier to pretend." This was pretty much my religion. I'd tell myself that it was just easier to pretend. Pretend I had money. Pretend that I wasn't in debt. Pretend that everything was fine. Pretend that I had it all under control. The problem with pretending; it isn't real. And pretending never feels good. At best, you'll just feel "pretend good." What I've seen, for myself and for my clients, is that pretending isn't easier at all. In fact, it's way harder. It's way harder to live with anxiety and guilt. It's way more difficult to constantly be pushing your feelings aside. It's way more difficult to lie to yourself.

"It doesn't matter." Telling yourself this lie will rob

you of your own happiness. Minimizing suffering never fixes it. Recognizing the truth is the only way to permanently eradicate your suffering.

Trust, honesty, respect, communication.

These are fundamental elements of a healthy relationship. And this applies to your relationship with money as well.

If you want to repair any damage, or strengthen the relationship, or deepen your understanding of money; it is crucial that you begin to tell the truth.

To yourself. About your money.

If you want to have a better relationship with your money, you'll need to let go of any old beliefs that justify avoiding the truth.

It's not too late.

It does matter.

And you are worth it.

Chapter 6

Beliefs That Enable The Discovery of Truth

We all have a breaking point. A rock bottom. A last straw. Some of us are smart enough to change course before we hit that point.

I am not one of those people.

I am stubborn. Self-righteous. Denial expert. Story-spinner-extraordinaire.

I would love to tell you that I was on the path of self-realization. That I was working on my own spiritual enlightenment—and came to these beautiful truths about money. I would love to tell you that my relationship with money changed due to my intelligence, my inner peace, and my amazing-ness.

But that's not the truth. After years of mistreating my money, it finally walked out on me. It had-had enough. And hit the road.

In other words. I was broke. For the first time in my life.

And not just a little broke. Broke and broken.

I had no other choice. I was either going to give up (never) or radically change my approach to money.

I knew that I needed to start with the truth. Figure out how and why I ended up where I was. And then, belief by belief, start building a new infrastructure for abundance.

The same is true for you. Our financial results depend on the thoughts that we believe. If we believe thoughts that avoid the truth, we will never create lasting abundance in our life. We will never be free from anxiety and worry.

So, I'd like to help you skip that whole "hitting rock bottom" part. You can start improving your relationship with money. Starting today.

Belief-by-belief, we can start building a foundation for a healthy relationship.

Here are some of the beliefs that my clients and I use to enable the discovery of truth.

Numbers are neutral. I probably say this to my clients at least a hundred times during our work together. And still...we forget. We think small numbers mean a better or worse thing. We think red numbers are bad. We think black numbers are good. We think big numbers are great when we're being paid and horrible when we're the one paying them. But this isn't the case. Numbers are always neutral. And only our stories about these numbers make them painful, neutral or wonderful.

Everything that happened was always meant to happen that way. This is a thought straight out of Brooke Castillo's arsenal. And I love it. It has helped me feel better hundreds of times. This thought has helped me through divorce, financial crisis, bad dates, family drama and even through writing this book. It's a keeper.

The truth creates more abundance in my life. Most of my clients are terrified of looking at the truth. They've never stopped to look at what lies really cost. There is no way to lie to ourselves or to lie to others and feel abundant at the same time. Lying just feels crappy. There's no way around it. When we live our truth, we feel better. And when we feel better we take better actions and create better results.

When I know better, I can do better. It's senseless to beat yourself up over past mistakes. We've all made them. There ain't one of us that has done everything perfectly. Instead of trying to hide or cover up your mistakes, be willing to look at them and understand them. This is a learning process.

You never have to recover from the truth. People are so afraid of telling the truth. Seeing the truth. Dealing with the truth. They tell themselves that they are afraid of the ramifications of coming clean. But that's not the case. You never have to recover from the truth. You have recover from the lies you have told. To yourself and to others.

If I know where I am, I will know the direction I should go. Knowing your financial status, in detail, is crucial for knowing the direction and actions you need to take to create different results. Physical and financial maps have no meaning if you don't know your current location.

The truth and anxiety cannot coexist. I love this thought. It has help me through so many anxious moments. We can only feel anxiety when we are believing anxious stories. And anxious stories are never real. They are stories about the future or about the past and they do not exist in reality or in this moment. The truth is neutral. It has no anxiety in it.

Questions for You

1. What does 'telling the truth about your finances mean to you?

2. Is telling the truth about your finances important to you? Why or why not?

3. What are you afraid to know or find out in this process?

4. What great news would you love to find out?

Chapter 7

Opening Your Eyes

Even when I was a financial wreck, I always had a pretty good idea of how much money I made. A foggier idea of how much money I actually spent. I could always give a rough estimate what my monthly bills came to. At the time, I thought I had a pretty good idea of what I could or couldn't afford.

Most of my clients think about their finances in the same way. They think in monthly totals. They think in terms of income and expenses. They think in terms of budgets.

And this type of thinking just doesn't give an accurate picture. Let me show you what I mean by this.

My client, Rachel, has been keeping a food and exercise journal for the past 30 days. Every day she wakes up and eats a small bowl of cereal, a banana and takes a multivitamin. For lunch she has sparkling water, a salad with light vinaigrette and sliced grilled chicken. For dinner she either has roasted vegetables and a piece of fish or she has a green leafy stir fry with brown rice. She doesn't eat dessert. She has given up sweets. She works out every day. She hikes every day for about 45 minutes. She does yoga 3 times a week. And she lifts weights with her trainer once a week.

Do you have a picture of Rachel in your mind?
How tall is she?
How healthy is she?
Do you know what size jeans she wears?
Or how much she weighs?

From this information you have no idea. You can form a mental picture, and you could make assumptions. But you do not know the truth.

When I add her height and weight, notice how much your perception changes. Notice how different your mental picture becomes.

Rachel is 5'4" and weighs 89 pounds. She has been keeping a food and exercise journal for the past 30 days. Every day she wakes up and eats a small bowl of cereal, a banana and takes a multivitamin. For lunch she has sparkling water, a salad with light vinaigrette and sliced grilled chicken. For dinner she either has roasted vegetables and a piece of fish or she has a green leafy stir fry with brown rice. She doesn't eat dessert. She has given up sweets. She works out every day. She loves to hike—usually for about 45 minutes. She does yoga 3 times a week. And she lifts weights with her trainer once a week.

What do you think of Rachel now? Is she healthy? Why or why not? What do you notice about her diet? Do you think this 30-day journal is representative of her typical nutrition? Why or why not?

Rachel is 5'4" and weighs 289 pounds. She has been keeping a food and exercise journal for the past 30 days. Every day she wakes up and eats a small bowl of cereal, a banana and takes a multivitamin. For lunch she has sparkling water, a salad with light vinaigrette and sliced grilled chicken. For dinner she either has roasted vegetables and a piece of fish or she has a green leafy stir fry with brown rice. She doesn't eat dessert. She has given up sweets. She works out every day. She loves to hike—usually for about 45 minutes. She does yoga 3 times a week. And she lifts weights with her trainer once a week.

What do you think of Rachel now? Is she healthy? Why or why not? What do you notice about her diet? Do you think this 30-day journal is representative of her typical nutrition? Why or why not?

Rachel is 5'4" and weighs 140 pounds. She has been keeping a food and exercise journal for the past 30 days. Every day she wakes up and eats a small bowl of cereal, a banana and takes a multivitamin. For lunch she has sparkling water, a salad with light vinaigrette and sliced grilled chicken. For dinner she either has roasted vegetables and a piece of fish or she has a green leafy stir fry with brown rice. She doesn't eat dessert. She has given up sweets. She works out every day. She loves to hike—usually for about 45 minutes. She does yoga 3 times a week. And she lifts weights with her trainer once a week.

What do you think of Rachel now? Is she healthy? Why or why not? What do you notice about her diet? Do you think this 30-day journal is representative of her typical nutrition? Why or why not?

With only a piece of the information (the 30 day journal) we can never really know the truth. We can't know if she's healthy or not. We don't know if this 30-day period was representative of her typical nutrition. In this example, her height and weight helped us make a more accurate assessment of her behavior.

Well, in the world of money, the equivalent of the scale is net worth. Net worth is our financial truth. It isn't just a 30-day snap shot. It shows the cumulative effect of our relationship with money.

A big income really means nothing if it comes with big debt and big spending. Many people with big incomes have little or no net worth.

When we focus on our monthly (or even annual) budget, we miss out on the big picture. We focus on the short-term and we take actions that can cost us dearly down the road. We don't see the long-term effect of our spending. Small amounts don't seem that significant. It's easier to justify extra expenses and to gloss over the impact of debt and finance charges. At best, this mindset will help you manage your income, but it can't help you build long-term wealth.

A net worth mindset frames things in a long-term perspective. Focusing on net worth takes us beyond simply managing from paycheck to paycheck, or month-to-month. Instead, the focus becomes building long-term wealth. We start to see the significance of small amounts over time. We clearly see the impact of debt on our bottom line. Net worth mindset is crucial for building wealth and is an indispensable tool for achieving financial independence.

Ok...we're going to start talking numbers here. Bear with me. I know this can be scary. Boring. Overwhelming. But trust me. I'm going to try to make this as simple as possible. I'm not going to get into complicated formulas or definitions. I'm not your accountant, financial advisor, or portfolio manager. I'm your money coach. And my job is to try to help make this as simple as possible.

In basic lingo, net worth is how much money you'd have if you cashed in and sold everything you own and paid off everything you owe. Think of it this way: imagine that you had to 60 days to move to China, you couldn't take a single thing with you. You sell your real estate, investments, businesses, and belongings at actual market value (not the price you paid). You sell your stuff through Craigslist, garage sales and Ebay for actual street value.

So now let's figure out how much money (or debt) you're actually taking to China. To keep it simple, I categorize my money into three categories: Money Makers, Money Takers, and Money Breakers.

Money Makers are things that you can sell for more than you paid. Also known as appreciating assets. Money Makers include savings accounts, IRA/SEP/401k, retirement accounts, investments, income properties, real estate (sometimes).

Money Takers are things that you can sell for less than you paid. Money Takers can include the current worth (street value today) of your TVs, stereos, computers, tech stuff, furniture, gear, motorcycles, RV's, boats, musical instruments, clothing, jewelry, or sports equipment. Money Takers also include the rest of the junk that you own that either can't be sold or would sell for next to nothing. This includes most of the stuff in your kitchen cupboards, bathroom drawers, and hall closets. It includes the stuff in your garage, storage sheds, holiday decorations, office supplies, guest rooms, almost everything in your kids' rooms, your linen closets, your book shelves, your dressers, and your closets.

Money Breakers are things that cost more than you paid. These are a double whammy because you lose your investment on the purchase and you pay more money to keep losing. These are things that cost more than they are worth because you buy them on credit and they lose their value. Money Breakers are anything that you buy with money that you do not have. Money breakers are car loans, school loans, credit card, retail cards, medical debt, dental/orthodontic debt, tax debt, business loans, personal loans, equity lines, line of credit, or some mortgages.

Some items are listed in more than one category. This applies to items that you have partially or fully financed. For instance, if you own a home with a mortgage, first figure out what you could sell the home for (What you would like to sell your home for isn't part of this equation. We are looking for actual current value). And then figure out what you owe on the house. The value of the home goes into the Money Maker category. The loan on the home goes into the Money Breaker category.

If you bought your car with a loan, list the value in Money Takers, and the loan in Money Breakers. If you bought a car with cash, the value is listed only in Money Takers.

To try and keep it simple: what it's worth goes into Maker or Taker (Don't get to hung up on Maker v. Taker. For the purposes of this exercise you can use either category). What you owe goes into Breaker.

To determine your **Net Worth** you need the total street value (in dollars) of your Money Makers, Your Money Takers and Your Money Breakers.

And now...deep breath...we are going to do the math.

Money Makers + Money Takers - Money Breakers = Net Worth

YOUR NET WORTH

List your Money Makers.
$475,000 if we sold our house right now
$25,000 401k
$1,000 savings
Total = $501,000

List your Money Takers.
$1,000 Furniture
$2,000 jewelry
$12,500 blue book on my car
$1,500 garage sale, ebay and craigslist everything else
Total: $17,000

List your Money Breakers.
$286 Victoria Secret card
$11,755 United Mileage Plus
$458 Macy's card
$385,400 Mortgage
$11,430 equity line
$14,670 car loan
Total: $423,999

Money Makers + Money Takers - Money Breakers = Net Worth
$501,000 + $17,000 - $423,999 = $94,001

My Net Worth is

$94,001

My client Angela has been tracking her expenses for the past 30 days. Her income includes her monthly salary ($7,000) plus her quarterly bonus ($5,000). Her monthly expenses include her house, her car, and day-to-day living expenses ($4,000). She always packs her lunch and never pays for gourmet coffee. Each month she pays $300 toward her Visa bill. She only shops at Target and Costco and prefers to buy things in bulk. She doesn't believe in having a high car payment. She tries to save as much as possible every month.

Do you have a picture of Angela in your mind? How healthy is her relationship to money? Do you think she is wealthy? Why or why not? Does she have a lot of debt? Does she live paycheck to paycheck? Does she have a lot of savings?

Similar to Rachel in the earlier example, we can't have an accurate idea of Angela's finances without more information. We don't know how much debt she has or how much she has saved. This is the way most of my clients try to manage their financial lives. They know only this much and they miss the big picture.

Now let's try again:

My client Angela has a net worth of $850,000 and has been tracking her expenses for the past 30 days. Her income includes her monthly salary ($7,000) plus her quarterly bonus ($5,000). Her monthly expenses include her house, her car, and day-to-day living expenses ($4,000). She always packs her lunch and never pays for gourmet coffee. Each month she pays $300 toward her Visa bill. She only shops at Target and Costco and prefers to buy things in bulk. She doesn't believe in having a high car payment. She tries to save as much as possible every month.

What do you think about Angela now? How healthy is her relationship to money? Do you think she is wealthy? Why or why not? What do you think about her debt? Her savings? The way she spends her money? How does her net worth change the overall picture of her finances?

Now try this one:

My client Angela has a net worth of $399,250 and has been tracking her expenses for the past 30 days. Her income includes her monthly salary ($7,000) plus her quarterly bonus ($5,000). Her monthly expenses include her house, her car, and day-to-day living expenses ($4,000). She always packs her lunch and never pays for gourmet coffee. Each month she pays $300 toward her Visa bill. She only shops at Target and Costco and prefers to buy things in bulk. She doesn't believe in having a high car payment. She tries to save as much as possible every month.

What do you think about Angela now? How healthy is her relationship to money? Do you think she is wealthy? Why or why not? What do you think about her debt? Her savings? The way she spends her money? How does her negative net worth change the overall picture of her finances?

Now it's time for you to figure out your own net worth. I know it seems tedious and it might even seem daunting. But if you really want to change your relationship with money, this is necessary work. The more detailed and accurate you are, the more solid your understanding of your financial life. I suggest making time for this. Take out all of the bank statements. Write down your answers to the penny. Do yourself a favor: don't fudge the details or skip parts of this exercise.

Remember: your net worth is just a number and numbers are neutral.

Questions for You

1. List and total all of your "Money Makers". These are the things that you can sell for more than you paid for them (Savings accounts, IRA/SEP/401k, investments without debt, income properties).

Name/Description   Cash Value

2. What thoughts do you have regarding your Money Makers?

3. List and total all of your "Money Takers". These are the things that you can sell for less than you paid (TV, stereo, computers, tech stuff, furniture, gear, toys, motorcycle/car/RV/boat with no debt, musical instruments, clothing, jewelry, equipment, etc.). Total all the other stuff, the things that you can't really sell, because it doesn't retain its value. Kitchen stuff. Pantry stuff. Refrigerator stuff. Cleaning stuff. Bathroom stuff. Garage stuff. Storage stuff. Shelf stuff. Holiday stuff. Technical stuff. Office supply stuff. Guest room stuff. Kids stuff. Linen stuff. Jewelry stuff. Clothing stuff. Make up stuff.

Name/Description   Actual Street Value
                                    (Craigslist price)

4. What thoughts do you have regarding your Money Takers? What thoughts do you have regarding your Stuff? How much do you think you originally paid (total) for your Money Takers?

5. List and total all of your "Money Breakers". These are the things that cost you more than you paid. (All credit cards, retail cards, lines of credit, student loans, property loans, mortgages, car loans, business loans, medical/dental/orthodontic loans.)

Name/Description   Pay-off Amount

6. What thoughts do you have regarding your Money Breakers?

7. Figure out your Net Worth.

Money Makers + Money Takers - Money Breakers = Net Worth

_____ + _____ - _____ = _____

8. What thoughts do you have regarding your Net Worth? What feelings come up for when you look at your Net Worth? Is it what you were expecting? Why or why not?

Chapter 8

What's Done
Can Be Undone

A few hours ago I had written the most brilliant chapter ever. It was witty. It was inspiring. It was personal. It was honest. It had all the good stuff that chapters should have.

It would have dazzled you.

It was titled, ironically, "What's Done Can be Undone"... just like this one. It was about how to deal with the truth of your net worth. How to avoid going into a catatonic coma after seeing your net worth on paper. How to come to terms with your financial reality. It was about the decisions we make and how we dupe ourselves into believing a story that we are stuck with our decisions. It was about learning to find the courage and freedom to change our minds. It was about making choices with our present lives that are valid to our current selves... instead of living with past choices out of regret, guilt, or fear of disappointment.

And of course, I have no proof of the geniusness that I shared on the page...because instead of clicking save, I accidentally pressed delete.

Noooooooooooooooo!
That didn't just happen.
I spent days on that chapter.
I'll never get it back.
@#$@%@#!!!

Not only did I have a freak out for about 40 minutes...but in that space of time I also missed a client call and was almost late for my daughter's recital. I got a stomach ache. And a head ache. I missed my workout. I decided that I should never have started writing a book. I considered giving up my profession. Packing up and walking away. Hanging my head in shame.

All this drama because of one little button on a computer.

And what I made it mean.

Somewhere in the middle of watching my daughter singing Winter Wonderland at her school assembly (and trying to re-write this chapter in my head), I saw the humor of the title. And the fact that what was done was undone.

The whole point of what I want to share is that everything can be undone.

And it's ok.

Duh.

So, this chapter has none of the brilliance, charm, and wit of the first draft. But it is about what really happened. And it's how I have learned to deal with things that happen. And it's how I help my clients work with things that happen.

The truth is: everything can be undone.

And re-done.

And undone. And re-done again.

Nothing in this world is truly static.

If you have regrets about decisions that you've made in the past. It's never too late to change. It's not too late to do what's right for you now.

What really matters is what you make it mean.

What I've noticed about this universe: I'm not in charge of how it runs. Sometimes things just happen. Sometimes housing markets crash. Sometimes people lose their jobs. Sometimes things break and need replacing. Sometimes you click delete instead of save.

And when we try to hold on to the universe and try to make it behave, we end up feeling powerless and stuck.

When we tell ourselves:

We should have never bought that house in 2006. We shouldn't have used those credit cards.

We should have saved more. We should have never left that job. Or we should have left a long time ago. We shouldn't have bought that. We should have returned this.

If you make your decision mean that you are stuck, a failure, no good or stupid...then you will be stuck forever. We don't have a time machine and we cannot change our past.

The only freedom we have is in this moment.

Right now.

We can choose a different path.

We can choose to let go of past decisions.

We can choose to undo what has been done.

Chapter 9

The
Abundance Scale

There have been very few moments in my lifetime that definitively and completely changed the trajectory of my life. Of course, most moments in life have this capacity, but in general, when I look back over my life to date, my top life-altering moments can probably be counted on one hand.

One of the moments on this short list was the first time I was shown how my thinking created my feelings.

Until then, I was stuck in a mind that believed its own stories. I didn't know that I could question what my mind said. I didn't even know that my mind said things that weren't true. I had no concept of the bondage that I was experiencing by my own hand.

In tandem to this, I really had no recognition of what an emotion really was. I only really knew if I felt bad or...not bad. I knew what intense stress, worry or fear felt like. And I knew the absence of that.

Words like happiness, peace, calm, joy, jealousy, regret and boredom really only had a conceptual meaning to me. I knew, in my head, what they meant, but I had no idea what they felt like in my body.

Most of the time I either felt bad or numb. Or badly numb. Or numbingly bad.

Up until that point, I didn't know that I could change my mind. That I could question my thoughts. That I could debate my beliefs. That I could find relief just by finding a new perspective. In other words, I didn't know how to get to the root of the problem.

Until then, I had only given myself two options: live within the painful stories of my mind, or try my best to numb and avoid my pain.

The trouble with emotional anesthesia is that it just prolongs our coma. It doesn't just numb the pain, it numbs all of our feelings. The good and the bad. Over time, we become sleepwalkers through a life of gray.

For most of my clients, "numb" is a way of life. It used to be for me as well. Some of my clients smoke, take pills, play video games, watch TV, Facebook, or work themselves into a stupor. My personal vices were drinking, eating, and shopping, or maybe even a mixture of all three.

This avoidant behavior was innocently intended to be a way to escape my negative feelings. To avoid my stress. To avoid my loneliness and stave off worry. But avoidant behavior never truly relieves these problems. It can push pause on the pain, but it doesn't help us process or recover. The real bummer about avoidant behavior is that it ends up creating the exact result we are trying to run from. When we're talking about money, the result we're usually trying to avoid is what we perpetuate: scarcity.

Since this is primarily a money book, we are

going to focus on money. Beliefs are the cause of money issues. Symptoms of these beliefs show up as debt, over-spending, under-earning, bounced checks, overdrafts, bankruptcies, foreclosures, job losses, and many other money-related issues.

But these are all just symptoms of the problem. If we focus on the symptoms, we will never get to the real cause. If we focus on the cause, we can create a solution that will permanently eliminate the symptoms.

To get to the root of the problem we need to know what we're feeling and what we're thinking. And the Abundance Scale is the tool that helps us do just that.

The Abundance Scale

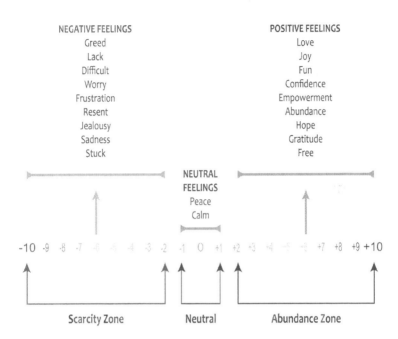

The Abundance Scale spans from -10 being the most scarce, most awful, most desperate feeling; 0 being neutral with no emotional charge, and +10 being the most generous, the most lucky, and the most secure feeling.

This tool is not an exact science. It's a tool to help you get to know yourself. It's a tool designed to show you that your emotions affect your results.

My goal is to help you eliminate worry, anxiety and fear from your financial lives. This tool will help you find sources of worry, anxiety and scarcity so that you can change your thinking to create a different result.

What are you feeling right now?

For starters just keep it simple. Do you feel good, bad or in the middle?

If you are feeling good, you would be in the abundance zone on the scale. If you are feeling bad, you would be in the scarcity zone on the scale. If you're in the middle, you'd be in the neutral zone on the scale.

Scan your body and try to give your feelings a name. Are you feeling glad? Relaxed? Agitated? Depressed? Amused?

Here are some common feelings and their

approximate value on the abundance scale:

ABUNDANCE SCALE

Joy, Love, Freedom, Gratitude	+10
Abundance, Generosity	+10
Empowerment, Fun	+9
Happiness, Enthusiasm	+8
Confidence	+7
Optimistic, Trust	+6
Strong	+5
Hope	+4
Dedicated, Motivated	+3
Content, OK	+2
Peace , Calm	+1
Neutral, Relaxed	0
Relieved, Apathy	-1
Pessimistic, Impatient	-2
Frustrated, Irritated	-3
Overwhelmed, Anxiety	-4
Boredom, Doubt	-5
Worry, Blame	-6
Discouraged, Difficult	-7
Anger, Revenge, Greed, Lack	-8
Hate, Rage, Jealousy, Resent	-9
Guilt, Insecure, Depressed	-10
Stuck, Fear, Grief, Self-loathing	-10
Powerlessness, Unworthiness, Shame	-10

What number on the Abundance Scale would you assign to your current feeling?

Right now, I'm at about a +8. I feel happy and confident. I got up really early to write. The house is quiet. I've gotten most of this chapter written before the sun has even come up. I have a great cup of coffee next to me. I'm excited about the rest of today. I have a full schedule of clients, a radio interview and then I will spend the evening with friends. I love my life. It's almost as good as it gets.

Even if you're not thinking about money. Even if you're not "feeling" about money. Even if you're worried because your neighbor's guinea pig is at the vet. Or you're happy because your niece just learned to walk. These feelings can be measured on the Abundance Scale.

Abundance and Scarcity are feelings. And there are many levels of intensity that can be measured with these two feelings. Scarcity is full of resistance. The more resistance, the more scarce you feel. It is a feeling of difficulty, struggle and stress. Abundance, on the other hand, is a feeling of harmony. The more abundance, the easier, happier, and smoother the feeling.

Even if your feelings have nothing to do 'with money'… they affect your money.

When you're stressed about your neighbor's guinea pig, what do you do? Do you take actions that build wealth—or do you take actions that stop wealth? If you're a business owner, I'm guessing that you're not launching new products, nor are you writing brilliant marketing copy, nor are you bonding with your clients. How could you with all that guinea-pig-stress? With that kind of stress most of us become counter-productive. We check Facebook, watch TV, eat, drink, and shop. These behaviors end up costing us…big time. Stress, even when it is only neighbor-guinea-pig-stress, still costs us.

When you're happy about your niece, what do you do? You smile. You share the story with people you come in contact with. You bubble over with enthusiasm and love. You might post something cute on your Facebook wall and get other enthusiastic people to comment. You have a little cute-fest in your life. This cute-fest may extend to your work, or it may not. You might be inspired to make a cute new product. Or you might send an email to that customer that came in with her baby a few days ago. The important difference here is that you do not engage in counter-productive or avoidant behavior when you're feeling abundant. And over time, the more abundant you feel, the more abundance you will have in your life.

Chapter 10

Four Types of Spending

I really never used to give much thought to my spending. In my mind, it was a means to an end. I liked paying for some stuff and hated paying for other stuff. I liked shopping and buying stuff. Especially stuff from Macy's, Nordstrom and Target. And, I hated paying for things like car repairs, taxes, and my retirement. But, I never really broke down how I felt about the actual spending of the money. The verb. The exchanging.

Instead, I focused on trying to make more money and tried not to focus on the spending. To be honest, thinking about my spending would just send me into a tailspin of feeling stupid, dishonest, entitled, childish and guilty. So, I did my best to avoid that subject.

Now, I give careful consideration to each money exchange and I help my clients do the same thing. We pay attention to how and why we spend our money. We recognize what type of spending that we're engaging in. We know where we are on the Abundance Scale. We recognize our patterns and deliberately keep our focus on the result that we are trying to relate.

We all spend money. We pay our bills. We pay the parking meter. We buy things. We go to the grocery store. We put gas in our car.

It's very rare to find a day that we don't spend money.

Each time money leaves our hands, or our debit cards, or our credit cards, or our bank accounts—we have an opportunity to learn about our relationship with money.

How we feel when we spend our money has an enormous impact on our financial results.

Our thoughts create feelings. From these feelings we take action. When we're talking about money, the actions that we take are spending and earning. These are the things we DO when we FEEL a certain way. The way we feel determines the type of action we take. When we feel neutral we take actions and create results specific to those actions. When we feel scarce, we take different actions and create a different result.

The tool we use for this is the Four Types of Spending. It's a tool to help you determine why you spend what you spend. It helps take the mystery out of your current finances. It helps you figure out why you ended up here in the first place.

Determining the Type of Spend strengthens your relationship with yourself and with your money. It's a tool that gives you an access point for cleaning up stressful and painful thoughts...even ones you never knew you had. It helps build self-awareness as well as financial awareness.

The Four Types of Spending are Abundant Spending, Neutral Spending, Scarcity Spending, and Avoidance Spending. Each type of spending leads to drastically different results.

Abundant Spending is money spent from the abundant zone on the Abundance Scale (+2 to +10). Thoughts about this spend are abundant, generous, and positively charged. You feel good about the price, feel good emotionally, and feel good about the item that you are paying for. It is an action that is taken from abundant and positive feelings and thoughts.

Neutral Spending is money spent from the neutral zone on the Abundance Scale (-1 to +1). Thoughts about this spend are neutral and not emotionally charged. You feel neutral about the price, feel neutral emotionally, and feel neutral about the item that you are paying for. It is an action that is taken from neutral feelings and thoughts.

Scarcity Spending: This is money spent from the scarce zone on the Abundance Scale (-2 to -10). Thoughts about this spend are scarce, resistant and negatively charged. You feel bad about the price, feel bad emotionally, and/or feel bad about the item that you're paying for. It is an action that is taken from a scarce and negative feelings and thoughts.

Avoidance Spending: This is money spent

unconsciously in order to not experience scarce / negative feelings and thoughts. Avoidance Spending is money spent in the scarcity zone on the Abundance Scale, even though you do not recognize the feeling at the time. This is an action taken to NOT FEEL something. To numb a feeling. This is an action usually taken to distract yourself from the truth. To distract you from what you're really feeling. It is typically money spent in order to avoid feeling broke, stuck, bored, lonely, punished or left out. Avoidance Spending can also be money that you are unconsciously spending because you aren't dealing with your finances (extras like unused gym memberships, extra cell phone minutes, unused automatic payments, overdraft fees etc.)

The Type of Spend is not price or item dependent. Many of my clients confuse this in the beginning. They think that inexpensive items are Abundant or Neutral Spends. They think expensive items are Scarce Spends. But, any time money is exchanged, it has the capacity to be any one of the Four Types of Spending. The Spend is determined by your score on the Abundance Scale (thoughts and feelings).

For example, let's look at how a cup of coffee can be all four different Types of Spending.

Coffee Scenario —Abundant

I am in a very good mood. I have plenty of time. I go to my favorite coffee shop, Kreuzberg, CA. Kreuzberg is a perfect place to hang out and get some work done. It's owned by one of my best friends, James, here in town. I walk in and I'm happily surprised to see my other two friends sitting at a table and talking. I join them. James brings me over the most perfect cappuccino (seriously...Verve...trust...try it) and sits down to join us. We all get caught up on the latest shenanigans and share out latest woes. These are my people and I love them. I drop a few bucks in the baristas' jar before I leave (because there's no way James will take my money). I feel great about my life, my time, my friends. I'm in a place of abundance—not just abundance of money but abundance of support, friendship, and care. I feel overwhelmingly grateful. Those dollars in the tip jar are an Abundant Spend.

Coffee Scenario —Neutral

I am on my way out of town and I want to grab a cup of coffee for the road. Right around the corner from my house is a tiny market that the neighborhood affectionately calls "The Pantry." I stop by The Pantry and grab a cup of joe. Not giving a lot of thought to the coffee or the price. I glance at the headlines on the newspaper by the cash register. Pay my two bucks and then hop in my car and head onto the highway. I'm feeling peaceful. This cup of coffee is a Neutral Spend.

Coffee Scenario —Scarcity

I have about 15 minutes before my next client and I'm exhausted. Maybe a cup of coffee will help. Ack! I'm out of coffee. There's a Starbucks a few blocks from my house over closer to the college and I decide to drive over there to get a coffee. There's a line to the door of college students. Every single one of them is going to be ordering a frappuccino. It's going to take forever to even be able to order my friggin coffee. I'm angry at the line. I'm frustrated by dumb college students who don't know what to order. I'm mad at myself for running out of coffee in the

first place. By the time I get to the front of the line—
I have exactly one minute before I have to be on a call
with my next client. I pay my two bucks and give the
barista evil eyes to try to make him hurry. I'm feeling
impatient and frustrated. Even though my thoughts
and feelings are not specifically about the money, this
is a Scarcity Spend.

Coffee Scenario —Avoidance

I wake up with a pit in my stomach. My little
girl is going on vacation with her dad for an entire
week. This is the first time that she's been gone this
long. I'm going to be dropping her off at school in an
hour and will need to say goodbye there. I hate this. I
decide to take her to the donut shop to celebrate our
last morning together. I get coffee and she gets a
donut and milk. We spend our last 15 minutes together
talking about her trip. I drop her off at school and get
back into my car and cry for the first time all morning.
I go to journal my spend and notice that I want to say
this spend was "Abundant" because it was a
celebration. But, the truth is that I was sad. I was sad
and trying to avoid being sad. I lied to myself and
called it a celebration. A celebration of what? Saying

goodbye?! That's nothing I like to celebrate. I tried to avoid my sadness by "celebrating." This is an Avoidance Spend.

Client Examples—Abundant

Client #1 - Money spent on my training course. I think it was the best thing I ever did for myself. I also love going to Starbucks for a nice Americano with cream and sugar and sitting outside and listening to the birds sing, the soft breeze blowing and the people walking by and enjoying the day. I really like to buy nice clothes or little things for my daughter. It makes me happy and she appreciates it. I bought Christmas gifts for two members of a family that the parents had lost their jobs. This was a program going on from the town I live in. I liked shopping for them and hoped they liked their gifts. I guess it's anything that gives me the "woohoo" feeling.

Client #2 - This idea of abundant spending is a precarious one for me. Once I really analyze where I thought the abundant spend was coming from, sometimes it ends up being scarcity. It is challenging for me right now to think of any spending coming from an abundant place. Yesterday, I took my kids to breakfast at this little coffee shop. I suppose going to the coffee shop and buying them breakfast there was abundant. I felt happy and we had fun. Paying for my kids' activities, acting classes, voice lessons all feel good. Taking them fun places feels good.

Client Examples—Neutral

Client #1 - The only kinds of things I could think of were things like utility bills. These are bills that come in every month. They aren't a surprise. We know generally what they'll be and they don't really make me feel a plus or minus on the scale. They just are what they are and I choose to pay them because I like lights and heat and A/C.

Client #2 - Getting my car washed. In general, going to the grocery store. Paying our regular bills. Writing a check for something to do with either one of my children's schools. Paying a co-pay at the doctor's office. Buying gas. I think of these things as neutral spends because no strong feelings, one way or another, come up. These are the sort of things that kind of need to happen and I am used to doing but they don't bring me any real joy or sadness. They just are. I am starting to equate neutral spending with things that are routine or repetitive and of necessity.

Client Examples—Scarcity Spends

Client #1 -The first thing that came to mind is when I needed to go buy some clothes for an event that I had to go to. Because I don't enjoy buying clothes for myself I usually feel frustrated and irritable because I can never find anything that I think looks really nice on me. Then I just resent spending the money on whatever it is. I also don't spend money on myself because I think it's a waste. It would be better if I would make the effort to go shopping and actually put some thought into it instead of just buying something that I think to myself, "this is good enough." Then I don't like it, I wear it and I don't feel good in it.

Client #2 - Gosh, what isn't a Scarcity Spend in my life? An example that sticks out in my head is for my friend's 50th birthday this past fall. I was in charge of planning a trip to New York City for all of our friends for a long weekend of celebrating, dining and going to shows. I decided that I was going to buy each and every person a special gift for making the trip. I bought everyone a giant personalized canvas bag, had their name stitched on the front, filled the bag with all kinds of treats related to New York, had T-shirts made, had customized cocktail tumblers that said "Lisa's 50th" and just a bunch of fun things like that. I spent a ton of money on these bags and delivered them with champagne to each person's hotel room. It sounds like a thoughtful gesture but behind it was a lot of scarcity going on because I did not have the money to purchase all of these items so I charged them. I felt overwhelmed and guilty or self-conscious that all of these people made the trip to New York - even though it was for Lisa, I felt responsible for any inconvenience that they might have had and I felt I needed to "compensate" them somehow. What made this a Scarce Spend was the fact that I was buying something out of worry, self-consciousness and anxiety. They were all negative feelings, and I felt worse afterward because I spent money that I did not have. The whole thing feels so ridiculous to me now and I have regret about doing it.

Client Examples—Avoidance Spends

Client #1 - Let's go back to the clothing example. I might go to a store and find a top that fits me and comes in several different colors. I'll buy most of the colors so I have them and don't have to look for anything else. Then when I have them at home I may just wear them because they fit or I might end up taking some of them back and returning them because the whole thing just makes me feel bad. I also have bought things when I feel like I'm in a happy mood and see something I think is pretty and I'd like to have, but then when I get it home I think, "Well, that's silly. Why did I spend the money on that? I'll never wear/use that." Then I take that back too. I also shop online for books from Amazon. I was spending several thousand a year at Amazon, purchasing clothes online. Sometimes, we eat out to avoid being home with ourselves. I'm pretty sure we spend way to much on car insurance, I've never checked.

Client #2 - I am thinking hard about this one. Going back in time and really thinking about my spending... I think a big chunk of my avoidance spending is on day-to-day things. I think about all of the little "errands" I create for myself during the week, or used to create, that involved spending money. A typical sort of avoidance spend would be: I need to go to Target for... but I would get there and buy all sorts of things that I didn't really go for in the first place. Like, toys, videos, books, household things... before I knew it, I spent $300 and it was one of my "errands." Or, going to a store to get candles for the house that I "need." I would treat it like an errand, or something I had to do, to feel better. Or I would use buying things for the kids as a way to spend and avoid. Going to clothing stores or kids stores and buying them things to add to their wardrobe and telling myself they need them. I really can't think of what I was feeling at the time... I have absolutely no idea. I now think these were avoidance spends because I am guessing that I was avoiding feeling bored, or like I had nothing to do etc. It gave me some purpose during the day and falsely made me feel like I was accomplishing things. It also temporarily lifted my spirits by acquiring things—and then going home to put them away.

In these client examples, you can see that the type of spend is not price or item dependent. The type of spend is determined by the way we are thinking and feeling. Any time money is exchanged, we have the opportunity to learn more about our relationship with money. Any time you spend money, check in with yourself. Figure out how you are feeling. Determine where you are on the Abundance Scale. Determine what type of spend this purchase will be. Become conscious of how you are feeling and what you are thinking.

Our goal is to feel as abundant as possible. It's our goal too think and feel as positive as possible about every monetary exchange. By doing this, you have the opportunity to create and experience abundance all day, every day.

Chapter 11

Three Types of Earning

I am so fortunate and incredibly smart (if I may say so myself) to have chosen a career that I like.

Actually, I don't just like it. I friggin' love it.

I love opening up my MacBook and checking my email. I love a full inbox. I love my clients. I love writing my blog. I love the students I train. I love answering emails. I love reading new material. I love creating classes. I love working on my website. I love invoicing my clients. I love "Notification of Payment Received." Best. Subject line. Ever.

To tell you the truth, I would do this job whether or not I was paid, because I love the work itself, but shhh… don't tell my clients that.

I love to kick ideas around with my colleagues. I love the challenge of a difficult thought. I love working from home in my yoga clothes. I love that I don't have to be pretty, have my hair brushed, or even have shoes on to make money.

I'm pretty sure I've made my point. But, for clarity, let's just say: I love my job.

After reading my little rampage, I'm guessing that you're either happy for me or entirely nauseated by me.

Either way, I want this love-fest for you, too.

Because if you don't friggin' love the way money comes to you, you're never going to reach your full earning potential.

How we feel when we earn our money has an enormous impact on our financial results.

We probably have 50,000 thoughts (I really don't know—I just made that number up) about the way we earn our money. What we think about our work, our job, our paycheck, the hours we keep, our bosses, our clients, our commute, our industry, has a giant effect on how and what we earn.

Our specific thoughts create feelings. The way we feel determines the type of action we take. When we feel neutral we take actions and create neutral results. When we feel scarce, we create scarce results. When we feel abundant we create abundant results.

To classify our earning, we use the Three Types of Earning. This tool helps us determine why we earn what we earn. It helps takes the mystery out of our income. It helps us figure out why we ended up here in the first place.

Determining the Type of Earning strengthens your relationship with yourself and with your money. It's a tool that gives you an access point for cleaning up stressful and painful thoughts...even ones you never knew you had. It helps build self-awareness as well as financial awareness.

The Three Types of Earning are Abundant Earning, Neutral Earning, and Scarcity Earning. Each type of earning leads to drastically different results.

Abundant Earning is money earned from the abundant zone on the Abundance Scale (+2 to +10). Thoughts about this earn are abundant, generous, plentiful and positively charged. You feel good about the amount earned, feel good emotionally, and feel good about the way you earned this money. It is an action that is taken from abundant and positive feelings and thoughts.

Neutral Earning is money earned from the neutral zone on the Abundance Scale (-1 to +1). Thoughts about this earn are neutral or peaceful, and without emotional charge. You feel neutral about the amount earned, feel neutral emotionally, and feel neutral about the way you earned this money. It is an action that is taken from neutral feelings and thoughts.

Scarcity Earning is money earned from the scarcity zone on the Abundance Scale (-2 to -10). Thoughts about this earn are scarce, resistant and negatively charged. You feel bad about the amount earned, feel bad emotionally, and/or feel bad about the way you earned this money. It is an action that is taken from a scarce and negative feelings and thoughts.

The Type of Earning is not amount or job dependent. Many of my clients confuse this in the beginning. They think that the higher the dollars, the more abundant the earn. They think that the lower the dollars, the more scarce the earn. But, anytime money is exchanged, it has the capacity to be any one of the Three Types of Earning. The Earn is determined by your score on the Abundance Scale (thoughts and feelings).

For example, let's look at how my income can be each of the three different Types of Earning.

Earning Scenario —Scarcity

I can't think of a current example, so I'm going to go back to college days when I worked at a cheap hotel. I worked the night shift—the worst hours for a 20-year-old's social life. My uniform was a nasty-polyester-flight-attendant-thing with a burgundy bow-tie. Boring doesn't even come close to describing this mind numbing work. I would stand (we weren't allowed to sit) and stare at the elevators for eight hours straight and stress about how much homework I had waiting for me at home (of course I wasn't allowed to do it at work even though there were stretches of hours without seeing another human being). I had a certifiably crazy boss who was convinced that I was the daughter that she had put up for adoption when she was 15. (Even though I told her that I'm pretty sure I'm my parents' biological child. She never believed me). I wish I was making this up. My paycheck was never enough to offset how much I hated this job. I hated the work, hated what I was paid, and felt totally stuck. This is Scarcity Earning.

Earning Scenario —Neutral

Every month I receive statements from my financial advisor. They are full of charts, graphs, and details about each retirement fund that I've invested in. I look through the pages and I see that some of the graphs went up. I'm not emotionally invested in this money. At least not yet. It's kind of interesting to look at, but at this point in my life, the gain doesn't have a lot of meaning to me. I have a neutral story about this earning. I don't feel emotionally charged about it. This is Neutral Earning.

Earning Scenario—Abundant

Amber is a super-fun client. She's funny, smart, and keeps me on my toes. She's sarcastic and quick and challenges me at every turn. I love working with her. She puts a lot of thought into her homework and asks great questions. When I see a response from her in my inbox, I'm always excited to read it. When I invoice her, she pays me immediately and with ease. I feel lucky to have her as a client. I am proud of the services I offer her. I am proud to be her coach and know that I am well worth the price she is paying. My thoughts and feelings about my work with Amber are abundant, positive and grateful. This is Abundant Earning.

Client Examples—Scarcity

Client #1 - So... this one is very familiar. All the money we have earned for the past 14 years has been scarcity earning. Even when our income went up, we were excited until we realized that even that would not cover, or would just cover our expenses. This includes both my husband's salary and my consultant fees because it always feels like it's not enough. We are constantly worried, disappointed, discouraged and fearful about our money coming in. I'm jealous of our friends because they don't seem to have the same struggle that we have. No matter what we do, it never seems like enough.

Client #2 - Our business income never feels like enough. It goes out so fast. It's been this way for the past several years. Our business has been a huge drain on us emotionally and financially. My focus was on our clients and our employees, we were not the priority. Every moment, I've been just trying to figure out how to stay open, make a buck, how to keep our jobs, keep everyone happy and pay the bills. It made me physically exhausted and overwhelmed.

Client Examples —Neutral

Client #1 - I don't have any from my current life. The time that feels neutral to me is when I was single and worked in a hospital. I earned a reasonable salary, way less than I could have earned in private practice, but I never thought about it. I more or less used it all up every month doing my single life thing, and never thought about it at all.

Client #2 - Neutral earning for me has been money coming from investments. Money from old accounts that I don't really use anymore. I guess money that I don't really know that I'm earning. I am usually happy about making money—so it's hard to think of a neutral earn.

Client Examples—Abundant

Client #1 - I remembered last night—when we sold our house—it was total abundant earning. It was a small house in a desirable neighborhood BUT it was on the busy street and very close to a major highway. We had renovated and made it beautiful. Still we had a low figure in mind due to location. The agent pushed us up a bit in our asking price. And people went wild! I remember sitting in our agent's office, and 14 offers coming in, one $75K more than asking. She still went back and told the top 3 to raise their offers. They came back higher and we sold for $90K over asking. I remember the enormous excitement and passion we felt. And how it stayed with us for so long. We felt so so lucky!

Client #2 - I feel that way towards my husband's paycheck. It's abundant and it always comes in. It is always a great surprise to see how much it is going to be. When I sell things on Ebay, I am in the abundant zone. When I have fun clients that I enjoy working with, I am in the abundant zone. Oh, and when I sell a book, I feel happy and that is super abundant.

In these client examples, we can see that the type of earning is determined by the way we think and feel. It's important to realize that how we think determines how we feel about the way we earn money. Too many people feel horrible, scarce and resentful about the way they earn their money. This is such a bummer, because every dollar they earn makes them feel even more broke. Scarcity earning does the opposite of what it's intended to do. The entire reason we earn money in the first place is to feel abundant.

Take a close look at the way you earn your money. Clean up any scarce, stressful or painful story about your earning.

Focus instead on feeling abundant and grateful.

Every dollar earned has the potential to be an abundant earn.

Abundance Cycle

Scarcity Cycle

Chapter 12

You Have Exactly What You Want

L ast week, a student in one of my classes, said that she didn't want what she had. To be clear, she specifically said she didn't want to be in debt. She didn't want to have financial struggle. She didn't want to be stressed about money.

And she was wrong.

She has the exact financial life that she wants to have.

And so do I.

And so do you.

This statement led to a half-hour coaching session as well as a week's worth of controversy on our class forum.

The way we feel boils down to the specific thoughts that we choose to think. And the thought, "I don't have what I want" creates struggle, stress and argues with reality. There is no way to find peace with this thought. It gives away your responsibility and your ability to change your life. And it gives away all of your power.

When you feel powerless, you become immobilized. When you feel like your financial life is beyond your control, you don't take measured action to create change.

And I know that this might be a pretty difficult concept to swallow at first. For most of us, it's way more fun to blame the economy, our husbands, our bosses, and my personal favorite: the evil credit card companies for our current financial lives.

But the truth is, we really do have the exact financial life that we truly want.

Here's why: Every thing we have spent money on was our very own CHOICE. Every little cent of it. We spend our money on those things because we WANT TO.

You may think, "But, I didn't want to pay my taxes, or my utilities, or my credit card bills." But that's not true. You wanted to pay for these things way more than you wanted to deal with the consequences of NOT paying. We choose to pay taxes over going to jail. We choose to pay our power bill rather than sit in the dark. Just as everything we've spent has been our choice, every dollar we have earned has been our CHOICE as well. We have chosen how, when, where and why we earn the money that we do.

We have the job (or not) that we have chosen to accept. We have agreed to be paid what we are paid. We are not victims of circumstance, we have made deliberate choices to be where we are. So, if we EARN what we want and we SPEND what we want...then we do end up having THE EXACT AMOUNT WE WANT.

This is good news. This gives us back our power to create a better life. It gives us control over where we are and what direction we want to choose from here forward. If we realize that our choices have created the financial life that we currently have, then we have the ability to change our future financial choices.

We can choose to spend less.
We can choose to make more.

When I asked myself this question: Do I have the financial life that I want to have? The answer was, "yes; this is the exact financial life that I DID want. And now I'm going to create the financial life that I know I'm capable of creating."

There's a beautiful poem by Hafiz that says:

This place where you are right now.
God circled on a map for you.

In that light, I'd say. This place where you financially stand right now. You circled on a map for yourself.

And from that place.
You can go anywhere.

Chapter 13

You Can't Buy Happiness

I used to say that I bought things because:

It was fun.
It was exciting.
It made me happy.
It felt good.
It gave me something to look forward to.

But, there was a problem with those answers. The problem was that my life wasn't fun. It wasn't exciting. I wasn't happy. I didn't feel good. And I had nothing else to look forward to.

Other than spending money.

My life was full of to-do's, obligation, and

monotony…with just a tiny sliver of freedom. And that tiny sliver was what I could buy. Target, Costco, Macy's, Sephora, Ann Taylor, Home Depot…if it had a cash register—it was my version of heaven.

If you asked me today, I buy things for a lot of the same reasons:

I still love to shop.

I still think it's exciting.

It's ridiculous how giddy I can be when I find a beautiful scarf or how I can die for pair of boots.

It still feels good.

And I still look forward to meeting up with my friends and going to our favorite boutique.

I still love fashion and I will continue to.

But, there is a distinct difference between who I was and who I am now. Now, my life is fun. It is exciting. I'm happy. I know who I am, and I fill my life with things that I love.

This wasn't always the case. I used to be…just blah. Unhappy with my life. Unhappy with my body. Unhappy with my marriage. With my career. With where I lived.

I felt completely stuck and tied down. I was trapped in the life I had created for myself.

Of course, I didn't recognize this at the time. I thought I was doing OK. I thought the way I felt was normal. Acceptable.

I tried to convince myself and train myself into wanting what I had. That is was good enough. I knew I had an aching desire for something…but I didn't know what it was. So, I'd push that ache down. Out of my consciousness. Set my jaw, and toughen up.

At the time, if you had sat me down and had a conversation with me, I would have said I was pretty happy. I had a little girl. Two houses—one in the mountains, one on the beach. A nanny. Gardeners. Housecleaners. A beautiful view. A husband. A career. All the stuff I thought I was supposed to have.

I had done everything right. Or so I thought. College, marriage, career, kid.

Even though I lied to myself and to the people around me, there was a part of me that knew there had to be more.

My mind was a broken record player, playing the thought "what needs to get done?" An awful question if you're looking to spice up your life. This question left me with nothing but confining lists, chores, and tasks.

My days were a string of sameness. The high point of my week was pushing my daughter in her stroller through Macy's. It was the closest I came to feeling free and alive. Which, is about as close as the North Pole is to Rome.

And that was the real problem.

The real problem was that my life had no substance. No authenticity. No connection. No real purpose.

The real problem was the loneliness that I didn't want to face. The disappointment that I didn't want to own. The lack of meaning and substance that I had allowed to infiltrate my life. The real problem was that I was not living my own life and felt completely invisible in the one that I was in.

The real problem was that my life had no joy in it. And instead of recognizing how painful it was to live that life, I numbed myself to the pain. I avoided the problem. And the problem just grew.

So, to try to give myself some relief—I'd head to the mall.

I know it seems ridiculous. What in the world could the mall fix? Nothing. But it pushed pause on my pain for a few hours—and at that time in my life, numb was as good it as got.

I had a problem with money because I had a problem with my life.

I wasn't living a life I liked. I wasn't living a life that I was proud of. I didn't know myself. My days weren't filled with things that I loved to do.

Most of my clients have similar stories. They feel like drones. Worker bees. They try not to ask too much from their life.

They live the same day over-and-over. Commute,

work, commute, TV, sleep.

They aren't learning or growing.
They have no genuine fun in their lives.
They have nothing to look forward to.
They have no authentic joy.
And, this is no way to live.

We don't create a mess of our lives because we are stupid. Or lazy. Or not good enough. Or unlucky.

We create this mess, simply, because we aren't happy. And we haven't learned how to deal with it.

What I've learned is:

No amount of spending will make an unhappy person happy.

No amount of stuff will make a lonely person feel connected.

No store will fill the void of emptiness of a boring life.

No purchase can give a hollow life purpose.

You can't buy honesty. Connection. Vulnerability. Security. Courage. Empowerment. Confidence. You won't find them on a shelf or in a bottle.

These are only things that you earn the old-fashioned way. From the inside out. Through your own self-work. Through your own willingness to be yourself.

I used to wait for life to happen to me. I was in a constant state of reaction. Trying to deal with what was slung at me.

Now, I happen to love my life. I actively create the life I want to have. I ask myself better questions like:

What's going to be fun today?
What can I accomplish here?
How can I make the best of this?
Who do I want to be?
How would I rather feel about this?

I intentionally fill my life with fun, happiness, connection, empowerment, and self-love.

This doesn't mean that my life now is purely roses and rainbows. There are plenty challenges that continue to come up. I still have days that bring me to my knees.

I still get frustrated. Sad. Worried. Scared. Angry.

But, now I know that avoiding these feelings only makes them stronger by weakening me.

Instead, I face these emotions head-on. I listen to the information that my feelings hold for me. I understand that my feelings help me create a better life. I look for the thoughts and beliefs that are causing my feelings. And then I do my thought work and find relief.

I no longer distract myself from my own life. I no longer run from, push away, or numb my feelings. I experience all of my feelings in vivid color.

I am living my own life. All of it. The life that I have deliberately designed for myself.

I know that money can't buy happiness. Because it's not for sale. It's created the old-fashioned way. By my own handiwork.

The only thing that can make me happy.

Is me.

Chapter 14

The Debt Cycle

I was 19 years old when I got my first loan. I was working my way through college and my old brown Mazda 626 had died. I needed a car, had no savings, so the only option I thought I had was to buy a car on credit at the dealership downtown. I called my grandma and she came down to co-sign. A 5 year old Nissan Stanza. 18% financing.

At that time, I was a full-time student. I worked at a hotel for $5.75 an hour. My rent was $185 a month and my car payment was $119 plus $95 a month for full-coverage insurance.

Never once did I consider an alternative.

Never once did I think there might be another way to go.

Debt was a way of life. It's how people got stuff done.

I was proud that I was building my credit score at such a young age.

I was proud that I was given a chance to make these payments.

I was proud of spending money that I didn't have.

In my twenties, I just began the process of trading up. A smaller car loan for a bigger car loan.

A smaller credit card for a bigger credit card.

Bigger student loans.

Bigger balances.

By the time I was thirty, I had access to the big loans. House loans. Lines of equity. Business loans. This was the late nineties and at that time it was easier to get a loan than a post office box. We began pulling money out of one house to buy another. We'd sell one, pay another loan down.

I never looked at my net worth. If I had, I would have seen my net worth was quickly dropping into red. I had no concept of net worth. I only looked at month to month.

I believed my own lies.

I believed that using credit was smart.

I believed that it would be easy to pay it all off.

I believed that this is was how to build wealth.

I believed that my husband and I would pay these loans off together over time.

I minimized the impact of the debt.

And the extent of the debt.

I thought this is how everyone lived.

And in my mind, the money that I had accessible on my credit lines seemed like my money. I didn't see a difference between my own money and money on credit.

In other words, I had no idea what cash really meant.

If you want to know how to get out of debt, you need to understand your answer to this question:

Why do you spend money that you do not have?

My clients will answer:

I needed to have something to live on while I built my business.

I would have missed out on the good deal.

I know I can pay it off later.

I don't want to give up the cash that I have. It's my safety net.

116

It's worth the additional fees and interest.

I use the miles from my card.

It would have been more expensive if I had waited.

It's an investment.

I didn't have a choice.

And all of these excuses will end up costing you a lot of money.

The only reason we ever spend money that we do not have is to avoid a feeling that we do not want to feel.

And if you can figure out what feeling you are trying to avoid, then you can make an informed decision as to whether or not it's worth it to purchase something to avoid that feeling.

We spend money that we don't have to avoid feeling—and inevitably it backfires on us.

The feeling we try to avoid is what we end up creating again and again through our debt.

We might spend money we don't have because we don't want to feel deprived. And by spending money on credit, all we do is deprive ourselves.

We might spend money we don't have because we want instant gratification and what we do is rob ourselves of long-term satisfaction.

We might spend money we don't have because we don't want to miss out on a deal and what we do is miss out even more.

We might spend money we don't have because we think we will find relief.

And that's a lie.

We aren't relieved at all.

Debt is not relief.

Instant gratification is not relief.

Staying in this compulsive cycle is not relief.

If you want to get out of debt, know why you spend money that you do not have.

List the reasons.

List the excuses.

There are a few among us who have a healthy relationship with money and who use debt as a tool.

Don't fool yourself into thinking you're one of these people.

Tell yourself the truth. Don't believe your own hype. Don't believe your own excuses. Cut through your justifications.

Ask yourself why would I spend money that I do not have? Study the answer to that question. Determine the validity of your reasoning. Look at the result that will be created by your actions.

I would never tell you or my clients, to cut up

your credit cards. I want you to understand why you use them in the first place. I want you to get honest with yourself and objective about your own reasoning.

This isn't about white-knuckling yourself out of debt. This is about understanding why you are there in the first place. It's about making different choices based on more honest information.

Once my clients understand why they spend money that they do not have, they can be more aware and more informed. From this place, there is no white-knuckling needed. They understand the ramifications of buying something on a credit card.

Chapter 15

Unlearning Our Lessons

I am the daughter of two glassblowers.

As a blower's daughter, I learned a lot about creativity, innovation, risk and courage. These lessons created the core of who I am, what I'm willing to do, how I work and what I'm about.

I also learned a lot about money.

Unfortunately, glassblowers are not notorious for their financial savvy. And the bulk of what I learned about money ended up creating a lot of financial strain in my life.

And even though you probably weren't raised

by glassblowers, you still had your fair share of money lessons. Some good and some bad.

We can't change our relationship with money without questioning these early money lessons. Many of these lessons have become our foundational beliefs about money.

To change our relationship with money, we need to determine whether or not these old beliefs are serving us. Whether or not these beliefs are true. And what it would mean to unlearn these lessons.

Here are a few of the lessons that I needed to unlearn:

There's not enough. There wasn't enough money. There wasn't enough opportunities. There wasn't enough orders. Or customers. There wasn't enough time. There wasn't enough…fill in the blank…that's the land that most of us were raised in.

Just like with all beliefs, we end up creating the exact result when we practice this thought.

When we think there's not enough, we feel scarce. When we feel scarce we take action from a place of lack. These actions usually include grasping, needy, clingy, hopeless and disempowered actions. And when we stack up those actions—we create the end result of not enough.

If we believe there isn't enough money—there won't be.

If we believe there aren't enough opportunities—there won't be.

Now I know that what I believe determines what I create for my life. At first, it was a stretch to believe that there is plenty. And sometimes, I just couldn't believe that thought at all. Sometimes it seemed like there was plenty for other people—but not for me.

So, this is the thought that I practice.

I choose abundance.

This thought reminds me that I have a choice in

what I believe. I might not have evidence at that specific moment, but I know that whatever I choose to believe ends up creating the life around me.

Since it's my choice…I choose abundance.

Money is a struggle. This was the religion that I grew up with. And it just isn't true at all. Our thinking about money can be a struggle. Not having money can be a struggle. Not earning money can be a struggle. Overspending money can be a struggle. In other words, what we do with money, how we use it, how we think about it, how we hurt ourselves with it (or by the lack of it)…those things can be a struggle.

But money itself is actually a pretty great thing.

If we believe that money is a struggle, then that's all it will ever be. We create our reality by our own beliefs. We prove our beliefs through our actions and create evidence with our results.

What I know now is that money is fun.

I enjoy money. It's exciting. I enjoy writing

about it, coaching about it. I enjoy earning it. I enjoy saving it. I enjoy spending it. It's fun for me.

You can't make money doing what you love. I used to think there were only two choices. Work at a job you hated and make money. Or do what you love and be poor. So many of my clients have this belief as well. They believe that security lies in the "real job." They work at jobs they don't love or even like because they believe that's the only place they can make a decent living.

And that's not living to me.

When I think of Oprah Winfrey, Steve Jobs, Dustin Hoffman, Jay-Z, I can see clearly how their passion, love, and inner drive created their success.

I do not need to sacrifice what I love, and neither do you. Success follows people who are willing to take risks. Who are willing to be themselves. Who are willing to do what they love. True abundance is created by doing what you love.

Money is meant to be spent. I never really

understood the concept of money. It was usually spent before it ever entered my hands. I had no respect for cash itself. Money only symbolized what I could buy with it. Here and now. Most of my clients are confused about the concept of money as well. They rarely pay attention to it. They rarely handle actual cash. They don't keep track of how much they have. They have no idea how much they want to keep.

Once I started telling myself the truth about my finances and began to understand my relationship with money, I had a better understanding of what to "do" with money.

I used to want to buy myself something. Now I buy myself some savings. I love having money in my bank. I love earning more than I spend.

Life would be better if we just had more money. I grew up thinking that money could solve anything. I believed if we just had more money, my dad would be healthier. My mom would be happier. They wouldn't fight anymore. My mom wouldn't cry anymore. I wouldn't stress anymore. My parents would love me more. My friends would like me more.

I really believed that what was between me and happiness was a bunch of dollar bills. And then I got a bunch of dollar bills. And I still wasn't happy.

Now I know that when you have more money, you just have more money. Life still happens all around you. What you make it mean is up to you. The way you feel is determined by your thoughts—not by the cash, or the body, or the husband, or the house, or the kids. It's determined by you, and you alone.

Life is better when we think better thoughts.

You have to sell out to become successful. There's no way you can be raised by hippy artists in the 70's without believing a fair dose of anti-authority philosophy. My parents taught me to do what I love. To follow my dreams. To not sell out. To not try to live within society's rules.

With one small caveat, I believed that to do this would mean that I would live on the fringe and pretty much be broke for the rest of my life.

I used to believe that if I tried to make money

doing what I loved, I would be a sell out.

Now I know that I am not for sale. And I do what I love. I own my own decisions. And I live the life I want.

And, I am successful.

I'm not one of those people. I grew up in a little cow town. There were people who lived on the hills on the west side in big houses with pools. I wasn't one of those people. I lived on the other side of town. We weren't the poorest. But we definitely weren't the richest either.

I come from a long line of people who struggled with money. If you trace my family tree, you will find fishermen and abalone shuckers. Modest people with modest jobs.

But, I've learned not to let my family or my past define who I am or my potential.

It doesn't matter where I come from.

It matters where I am going. I can be whomever I want. And so can you. Don't let your childhood beliefs stop you from creating who you really want to be.

Chapter 16

The Power of the Written Word

Imagine this. You're in a relationship and you have something that you really need to say. It's very important. Actually, it's more than important. It's urgent and critical and you're at your wit's end.

You know you need to have a talk. So you start up a conversation with your partner. Immediately, he just zones out. You see that familiar glazed-over look. He's not listening. He turns up the TV to drown out your voice.

He grabs a few beers from the cooler next to his La-Z-Boy and starts to chug 'em—hoping to make you go away. That doesn't work, so he goes into the kitchen to grab a bag of Doritos, stuffs a handful into his mouth, and chomps over your voice. You try to keep talking, but you realize that between the TV and the beer and the chips, you're never going to be heard. You know the pattern—because you've been living like this for years. You try to talk to him. He ignores you. He doesn't want to hear what you have to say. He's afraid of what you're going to say. So he does his best to turn up the TV and drink a beer—and hope you just go away.

This is the type of relationship that many of us have with money. And no, the money is not the dirt-bag husband in this story. Our money is the wife in this scenario. And we are the dude that's trying to avoid the conversation.

For any relationship, money included, communication is vital. We cannot have a healthy relationship with our husbands, our friends, or our kids without open and honest communication. And we cannot have a healthy relationship with our money without open and honest communication either.

If you want to know why you spend what you spend and why you earn what you earn, I suggest keeping an abundance journal. This journal will open up the dialogue between you and your money. Not in a woo-woo Ouija-way, but as an in depth study into what you think and feel about your daily monetary transactions.

The Abundance Journal is the single most important tool that my clients use to create permanent change in their financial lives. There is no better tool for helping you understand, dollar-by-dollar, your relationship with money.

Many money programs recommend writing down income and expenses and building a budget from those numbers. This is not at all what I want you to do, though.

The primary purpose of the Abundance Journal is to become aware of every time you spend money or earn money and the thoughts and feelings that we have about each transaction.

The reason people want more money is so that they can feel better. Journaling allows us to break down each line item and look for any thoughts or feelings that are creating stress, scarcity and anxiety. It allows us to determine where we were on the Abundance Scale and what type of earn or spend it was. With this information, we can start to see beliefs and underlying patterns.

It gives us the opportunity to create abundance line-by-line by changing our thinking.

I ask my clients to keep an Abundance Journal for 30 days. It is the single highest indicator of my client's success. And it is the tool that 99 out of 100 of my clients will skip.

People have thousands of excuses as to why they don't, can't, or won't keep a journal.

I'm too busy.
I'll forget.
I already pretty much know what I'm spending.
It's petty.
It will be too much work.
It will depress me.
I already track my expenses on Quicken.

(Insert picture of husband turning up the volume on the TV. Don't turn into this guy. Your money is trying to talk to you. Listen).

I'll tell you this: if you're willing to do this work—you will be amazed at how much you learn about yourself. And about your money.

To have an effective Abundance Journal you want to write down every spend and every earn. Every day. Include credit cards, debit cards, automatic payments, cash, coins…everything.

After each spend, determine where you were on the Abundance Scale for that spend. Determine which Type of Spend it was: Abundance, Neutral, Scarcity, Avoidance. And list any thoughts or feelings about that spend.

After each earn, determine where you were on the Abundance Scale for that earn. Determine which Type of Earn it was: Abundance, Neutral, Scarcity. And list any thoughts or feelings about that particular earn.

My clients who do this exercise are usually blown away by how they typically feel when money is entering or leaving their hands. Up until this point, they were unaware of how bad they usually felt about money. Or how unaware they have been.

When they begin journaling their spends, they usually start with very low scores on the Abundance Scale.

This work teaches them that every single time they spend money or earn money, they have an opportunity to feel horrible or great. Most of my clients come into this work thinking that they have to earn more money to feel better. They learn that by thinking better, they feel better instantly.

They can choose to feel better about the money they spend at the grocery store, the gas station, the restaurant, and at the parking garage. They can choose to feel better about paying for utilities, phone bills, medical bills and taxes.

And each time we choose to think more abundant thoughts about these things, we end up feeling better. In effect, we have the opportunity to feel abundant all the time. Without getting a raise. Without winning the lottery. By changing the way we think. Which costs nothing.

Here's an excerpt from the first few days of my client's Abundance Journal—and my coaching notes back to her:

ABUNDANCE JOURNAL
Client Example - first week of journaling.

Description	$ Amount	Abundance Scale	Type of Earning	Notes about Thoughts and Feelings
client income	333.10	-2	Scarcity	It just doesn't seem like enough money. I can't believe I'm still stuck in this same place...just waiting for the next client. Not knowing where my next money is coming from.

Spendings (Cash, Check, Credits, Trade)

Description	$ Amount	Abundance Scale	Type of Spending	Notes about Thoughts and Feelings
Gas bill	$196.10	-3	Scarcity	I hate spending money on things I can't really see. I can easily change my thinking on this - I love being warm in my house.
Taco Rocks	$14.80	-2	Scarcity	Poor quality food. I can't believe how often I eat out at places that I don't even like.
Hacienda	$45.85	-3	Avoidance ?	I was trying to save money by not going out to an expensive dinner. I didn't want to go home to just the normal same-ol-same-old so I got take out to bring home. The food was good - but way too expensive for what I got.
Starbucks	$4	-3	scarcity	I used this as a bribe to get my daughter to school. I shouldn't have to go to Starbucks just to get her out the door on time. Great parenting moment.
Supplies for school party	$15.25	-4	scarcity	I went in to get sprinkles. I was mad that I'm in the place that 4 bucks is such a big deal. I hate that I have to have these discussions with myself. I ended up buying the sprinkles plus other stuff that I didn't even need.

Description	$ Amount	Abundance Scale	Type of Spending	Notes about Thoughts and Feelings
Deposit for annual party	$200	-6	scarcity	Every time something like this comes up - I think I should be over the whole money thing by now. I shouldn't be stressing over $200
Hair cut/color	$185	-3	scarcity	I think it's expensive and I always stress about the tip. I think I really don't have the extra money for a tip, but I struggle with feeling rude if I'm not generous.
Website	$9.20	-4	Avoidance - didn't realize that I would be continually charged.	I guess I didn't pay enough attention to this. I thought I had paid for the entire year already. But now they are charging me monthly.

Coaching notes to client:

It doesn't matter how much money you earn, when it comes with a thought like "This isn't enough money," you will always feel scarce. And that is just an awful feeling. You may not have control over where your next client is coming from, but you do have control over what you believe about this payment. Try, instead, to find a better feeling thought about just this specific payment. Instead of thinking that it's not enough—try to reach for a thought like "every dollar matters."

There are a lot of things that we spend money on that we can't see. To keep this belief will be exhausting for you. I'm glad that you found other thoughts about this—and found a way to change this into an abundant spend.

It's amazing how many times we spend money and don't notice it; and on things we don't even like. That's why keeping this journal is such a valuable tool.

The Hacienda dinner looks like money spent to avoid the feeling of "same-ol-same-old." Spending money doesn't fix this. The feeling is there for a reason. This is an invitation to see what's really going on. If the problem is boredom—money (and food) is not the solution. Yes, this would qualify as an Avoidance Spend. Next time, let's try to find the awareness before the money is spent.

Regarding Starbucks and your daughter, just realize the urge to use money to try to solve your problem here. That $4 doesn't solve the problem, and it ends up creating an even bigger problem when you're spending more than you earn. I'm not saying that you aren't allowed to take her to Starbucks, of course you are. But there's a big difference between feeling generous and loving or feeling resentful and manipulative.

Regarding the party supplies—it looks like you went into buy something that cost $3 and ended up spending $15. Realize that this internal struggle with being mad about the state of your finances, ended up creating an even worse state for your finances. When we take action from a scarce place we create an even more scarce result.

Thinking "I should be over the whole money thing by now" is very stressful. I don't see an upside to this thought. For spends like this, let's see if we can find something more neutral, like "I am in the process of learning about money."

Let's talk about tipping. Tipping out of obligation will always be a scarce spend. Clean up the thoughts about the service being expensive, first. This is a service that you are choosing— and your choice to spend this money in this way can feel either abundant, neutral or scarce. I would never suggest spending money from a place where you think the service is over-priced or you feel obligated to tip. Clean up your thinking first. Find that it's your choice. And tip from generosity.

Regarding the website—when the spending is unconscious, it is classified as avoidance spending. This stuff adds up fast. This isn't something that you want to just ignore. Let's try to figure out what was going on (in your thoughts/feelings) that took you to the action of signing up for a year's worth of charges without realizing it. Let's also try to figure out how to eliminate this expense in the future (if you choose to do so).

ABUNDANCE JOURNAL
Client Example after one month of journaling.

Description	$ Amount	Abundance Scale	Type of Spending	Notes about Thoughts and Feelings
Cancelled magazine subscription	$19 a month	+6	Abundance - even though this isn't exactly an 'earn' I really feel like it is.	I've been meaning to do this for months. We hardly ever look at this magazine and it bugs me every time I see it on our monthly statement. No longer.
Client income	$281	+5	Abundance	I realize how much my own head has been getting in the way of my earning. I am so grateful to have my clients. I adore them.
Husband's paycheck	$2735	+5	Abundance	It's funny how this used to seem like it wasn't enough - and now it seems so abundant to me. I love being paid and seeing this deposit in the account.

Spendings (Cash, Check, Credits, Trade)

Description	$ Amount	Abundance Scale	Type of Spending	Notes about Thoughts and Feelings
Parking	0	+4	Abundant	Even though there was no money exchanged - I wanted to write this down. I would usually pay for parking begrudgingly. I don't do this anymore. We parked for free today. We walked a bit further - but I saw it as money in my pocket and it was so worth it.
Lunch + Cash back	$24.45	0	Neutral	No emotional charge. Loved the food - but just getting things done.
Groceries	$158.26	0	Neutral	Wanted to purchase more treats, felt scarce, then put some back until my feelings were neutral.
Cosmetics	$179.20	5	Abundant	Very abundant spend - I used to spend a ton of money on a very expensive line - and ended up not using most of it. Now, I buy what I want to buy - only when I'm feeling good about it. I always have a choice. I pay attention to what I'm buying. And I use what I purchase.
Bank service charge	$5	-5	Scarcity	Pissed. I still need to call and figure this one out. I'm realizing that the way I feel has nothing to do with the dollar amount. It's totally about what I'm thinking (duh). Before, I would have just dismissed it as 'only $5' and let it go. Now, I will call and ask them to remove the charge. My money is worth my attention.
Visa	$2000	-2	Scarcity	We aren't paying in full this month, which means we will be paying interest. Im a bit disappointed, but not frantic.

ABUNDANCE JOURNAL
Earnings (Cash, Check, Credits, Trade)

Description	$ Amount	Abundance Scale	Type of Spending	Notes about Thoughts and Feelings

Spendings (Cash, Check, Credits, Trade)

Description	$ Amount	Abundance Scale	Type of Spending	Notes about Thoughts and Feelings

Chapter 17

The Other Side of a Dollar

A lot of people believe they'd be happier if they had more money.

It seems logical...right?

I mean, doesn't it seem obvious that if you won the lotto, or got a raise, or inherited an unexpected windfall of moolah you'd probably be happier? Or, if you had more money in your checking account, or savings account, or less debt, you'd be happier, right?

Believe it or not...if you had more money.

You'd just have more money.

You wouldn't be happier.

You wouldn't be thinner.

Your marriage wouldn't be better.

Your kids wouldn't want to spend more time with you.

You wouldn't find your true love.

You wouldn't wouldn't be more loved.

You wouldn't be more popular.

You wouldn't be anything other than **you**...with more money.

It's so painful to think that our happiness resides on the other side of of a dollar sign. Thinking that we'll be happier if we make more money sets us up for mandatory suffering. I don't know about you, but so far, I haven't figured out a way to make the universe behave the way I want it to. So, if I truly want to be happy, I need to figure out a way to be happy in the universe that exists here and now. If I truly want to be happy, I need to figure out a way to be happy with whatever happens to be (or not be) in my bank account.

If I believed that my happiness depends on more money, then I'd be stuck in suffering trying to wrangle the universe into putting more cash in my bank so that I can feel better. And this just never works.

The truth is: nothing can make me happy except for me. What makes me happy is the perspective I take on my life. It's the story I tell myself about the universe around me. My happiness is determined by my discipline to find thoughts that feel good. My happiness is **my** choice—not my bank's.

Money can't make me feel anything. It can't crawl inside my body and produce emotion. It can't change the way I think. Only I can do that.

And money can't make you feel anything, either. Only **you** can do that.

Money on its own has no power over your emotions. Money is neutral. The **story** you have about money can create intense abundance, gratitude, love, and happiness and your story also has the power to create incredible suffering, worry and anxiety. But money...cold hard cash...has zero power over the way you feel.

If you want to be happier...you have to start with you. Don't set yourself up to think, "If I had more money, then..." because the truth is, "If I had more money, then **I'd give myself permission to believe** something that makes me feel happy or secure."

So, if you want to be happy. Then be happy, now. Don't wait for the magic number on your bank statement. Don't wait until the debt is gone. Don't wait for the bonus, or the raise. Don't wait. Think about things that feel good in your life right now. Find ways to feel grateful about the opportunities you have. Find ways to feel loving about the people around you. Find ways to express joy, hope and excitement about your life right now.

Happiness truly costs nothing.

Chapter 18

Money and Me

My relationship with Money has had some pretty dramatic ups and downs. And when I say dramatic, I mean the Jerry-Springer-style-trailer-trash-call-the-cops-this-woman-is-off-her-rocker kind of drama. Money and me? We've been through it.

I've done all the things that horrible partners do. I've treated it awful. I've ignored it. I've pushed it away. Lied to it. Abused it.

At the same time, I've held it up to ridiculous standards. I've expected it make me happy. To complete me. To take care of me. To make me feel safe.

I've fantasized behind its back. I've cheated on it. Took it for granted. Used it as a source of torment and worry. I've given very little back. I've told countless stories about how I am pure and innocent and how I've been victimized by this evil perpetrator.

I've held it at arms length, turning my nose up to it, thinking I was superior. While being desperately needy and terrified it would leave me. Secretly hoping that I could either beat it into submission, or guilt it into staying with me.

I don't know a single relationship that could weather this type of abuse. Day in and day out. For years upon years.

Even Money has its limits.

Money had every right to file for divorce, to leave me for good and never look back. I had been blind to my dysfunction, my neglect and my responsibilities within the relationship. I was left with just me and my stuff. All the remnants of my dysfunctional relationship. It took a giant wake up call through separation to open my eyes. To see myself. To see Money. To see the truth.

The more I started to tell the truth, the more I could see my part in the relationship. The more I could see the effects of a lifetime of neglect. The more I could take responsibility for my behavior instead of feeling like a victim of circumstances.

I realized that I couldn't have a healthy relationship with Money until I had a healthy relationship with me. I began working on my mind, my thoughts and my beliefs. I worked on the patterns of dysfunction and found a deeper, better understanding of myself. I had compassion for the raving lunatic that I once was in this relationship. I forgave myself.

And so did Money.

As with any damaged relationship, starting over is tentative. Slow. Cautious.

Trust is built over time. It's built on the foundation of honesty and awareness. It requires a practice of doing what I say I'm going to do. Being who I say I am. Following through with my commitments. It requires self-reliance to my own integrity, strength and ability to create a healthy relationship with myself and with money.

It requires deep self awareness. Intimately knowing myself, my thoughts, my beliefs and my emotions. Understanding why I do what I do. Having compassion for situations that appear to be mistakes. Having the patience to keep learning.

It requires taking responsibility for the richness of my life instead of holding Money accountable for a job it's ill-equipped to do.

These days, I treat Money a hell of a lot nicer. I pay attention to it. I check in with it. I respect it.

Of course, I'm not perfect. This relationship is still a work in progress. But, when I screw up, I take a good long look at what I've done. I figure out why I did what I did. I practice kindness to myself and to Money.

I tell the truth. To myself. And to others.

I love everything about Money. I love making it. I love spending it. And, I love keeping it around.

I love hanging out with it, thinking about it, and understanding it. I love taking care of it and watching it grow.

I love helping my clients repair their relationship to it and teaching others how to love it.

I love Money.

And I have found that Money loves me back. And with a little bit of self-trust, inner-forgiveness, and practiced awareness, it will love you back, too.

Chapter 19

Money Love

Our relationship with money is not a frivolous thing. Money is a force in our life, whether we like it or not. It's nearly impossible to live a life without money interfering or assisting in some way or another.

Your relationship with money isn't determined by luck or by chance. It's determined by you. By what you believe. Money can be your friend or your enemy. It's up to you to decide to do the work required to strengthen your relationship to your money and to yourself. To repair any damage. To open your eyes to who you really are.

You might think you can run from yourself. Or that you can put this work off. Or that you can do this work later. And you're right, you can run for a while. You can hide, pretend, cover your eyes. But, doing this will only postpone the inevitable.

To repair your relationship with money means to repair your relationship with yourself. And that can be daunting. Especially if you don't know who you are. Or what you want. Or what brings you joy. Especially if you've long silenced that inner voice who asks, "Please?"

But you are worth this work.

You are worth knowing.

You are worth Money Love.

Money Love means knowing yourself inside and out. It means understanding why you do what you do. It means knowing that your thoughts lead to your results. It means deliberately choosing beliefs that support the results you want to attain.

Money Love means telling yourself the truth. About everything. Even the yucky stuff. It means being willing to risk being yourself. And showing up.

Money Love means being at peace with money. Being proud of your money. Having integrity with your money.

Money Love also means being at peace with what you owe. Being willing to forgive yourself. Being willing to keep your promises. It means being at peace with what you've done with your money in the past. And having compassion for the current state of your relationship.

Money Love understands the strength of the big picture and the power of the small transaction. It understands that even one dollar has the potential to create abundance or scarcity in your life if you let it. It understands that each transaction affects not only your financial net worth but your emotional net worth as well.

Money Love means deliberately finding an abundant perspective on anything that you choose to give your money to. It means doing the thought work required when you feel scarce, or scared, or worried and choosing instead to feel grateful, generous, or empowered.

Money Love means taking a good long look at the work you do in this life. It means not tolerating negative thinking about the way you earn your money. It means telling a better story about the way your money comes into your hands. It means loving your work, and loving to get paid.

Money Love means loyalty to your money. It means that you only spend money that you actually have. It believes in cash and understands what a dollar stands for. It means spending money only on things that you really want. It means that you no longer spend for spending's sake.

Money Love means going into Target, Costco, the grocery store, or Nordstrom and staying present and conscious. It means walking through any store without the shame of a junkie. Without feeling deprived. Without feeling naughty or untrustworthy. It means walking into any store and knowing what you really want. And knowing that spending money, especially money that you do not have, can never create what you're really wanting. It means knowing that your mind, alone, has that power.

Money Love knows that the worst thing that can happen is an uncomfortable emotion.

Money Love means that you will make mistakes. Even big ones. It means allowing yourself to make these mistakes, eyes wide open. To watch yourself doing the very thing you wish you weren't and to stay connected to the present moment. To stay there with yourself and with your money. And to observe with the curiosity of a bright-eyed student.

Money Love knows the journey ahead of you can be hard. That it might strip you naked. Exposing who you are to life itself. It knows that healthy relationships take work and that this work is worth doing.

Money Love doesn't give up. It doesn't quit, even though it sometimes wants to. It doesn't expect the road to be easy. It appreciates the journey and doesn't believe in the myth of a destination.

Money Love knows that relationships thrive on trust, communication and love. It expects that there will be times where faith and trust have been lost. It also knows the solid foundation that is built from allowing this bond to be broken and mended. And then mended again.

Money Love is found at the unshakable center of your life. It's found at the core of who you are. It is found in the place where you drop all pretenses and look at yourself.

And like what you see.

And smile.

I want this for you. I want you to know the freedom on the other side of worry. I want you to know how it good it feels to drop the dysfunction and to start to love again. I want you to know that money isn't your enemy. It isn't against you. It hasn't forsaken you. No matter what you've done or believed in the past, this relationship, between money and you, can be better. Stronger.

It might take some time. It may take quite a bit of effort. It will probably take a helluva lot of practice and some pretty radical self-awareness.

But, do this work.

Money Love is worth more than any price you pay to find it.

And so are you.

Made in the USA
Lexington, KY
14 July 2011